Breaking into the Art World
How to start making a living as an artist

By Brian Marshall White

Published by

Virtualbookworm.com Publishing

Cover art by Marshall White
©2000 Marshall White Fine Art

Title of art:
Art World/Determination

This painting is a self portrait and was made just prior to
my leap into the art world full time. It expresses my frustra-
tion with the art world system, a system designed for artists, and yet seems also made to keep artists out. It also
expresses my determination to break in against all odds.

ISBN: 1-58939-762-2

Published by
Virtualbookworm.com Publishing
www.virtualbookworm.com
P.O. Box 9949
College Station, TX 77842

Dedicated to
Pamela Jean White
My friend, soul mate and loving wife.

In gratitude

To the living God, my creator and Master artist of all
artists.

My wife, my Children, Mom & Dad and Aunt Jan
*For their love, encouragement, guidance and support
through the good times and the hard times.*

Randy Nagle
*Long time friend and fellow artist, a kindred spirit,
who's work I admire.*

Robert Thomas
*A great artist, teacher at heart, and friend. For sharing
information and being an inspiration.*

Doug Heck
Long time friend who taught me leadership and business ethics.

Mike McLaughlin
For teaching me to strive for excellence.

Ralph Osborne at Hula Bean Coffee.
*For his friendship and letting me paint in front of his
store. A gracious act that not only was a major part of
launching my art career, but also kept me and my family from starving.*

Ron & Kathy Fuchs
*For being best friends, encouraging us and supporting
us in every way.*

The question has often been asked;
"Can you make a living as an artist?"

Breaking into the Art World
How to start making a living as an artist

Introduction

First of all I'd like to say that breaking into the art world to become a full-time artist has been one of the most difficult and confusing things I've ever tried to do. I've been an artist since my childhood, drawing and painting as hobby, but it wasn't my skills at art that kept me from making a living with my art... It was not knowing how to get started.

As a self taught artist, and no formal education to back me, galleries wouldn't consider me without a prior track record of sales, and, I couldn't have sales unless a gallery would carry my work.

Everyone I talked with had different answers to my questions on how to get started. Most only suggested I find a famous local artist and offer to clean his or her brushes in exchange for learning how to paint. This didn't help. I knew how to paint. I needed to know how and where to sell my art.

Stories of starving artists who had made a name for themselves and at the same time had lost spouses and their children because of their life of poverty were everywhere. I wasn't willing to make this kind of sacrifice, so my desire to make a living doing what I love was put on hold for years until I finally found a way to make a living with it. Then I took the leap of faith and went full-time.

For years I compared my art skills to the skills of other artists who were selling their art in galleries and shops. Many of the ones I looked at had exceptional skills, but there were many more of them who had less talent than I did, and yet they were making a living with their art. If you are an artist, you know what I'm talking about. You walk into a gallery or gift shop that sells art, you look around and say "I can do that," or, "my work is better than that," and you think to yourself, if they can make it as an artist why can't I ?

What is the difference between me and the artists I see in the galleries and gift shops? They have their work on display and it is available to buy. I on the other hand have my art hanging on my living room walls. No one sees it, and no one knows I have it for sale.

At the completion of this writing, it has been four years since I started full-time working as an artist, and I believe I have found some key elements that will help you get started in your own art career.

In this book I won't be talking about painting and drawing techniques. However, I will be sharing with you information on how to get started marketing and selling your art. I will also be giving you information about reproducing your art and some resources for obtaining the materials you need to do so.

I will be sharing with you a way to get started that has worked for me and I will also share some dos and don'ts to help you avoid some pitfalls along the way. This is by no means the only way to get started, but I think that the information you glean from this book will be valuable in helping you understand how the art world works and how you yourself can get started reproducing, marketing and selling your own art.

Many of the things I've learned have come from my own experiences and talking to other artists who have been open and willing to share information with me.

The question has often been asked;
"Can you make a living as an artist?"

The answer is *YES*, you can.

Brian Marshall White

Table of Contents

Chapter One
Building a Base Income

If you are going to survive as an artist, you will need an income to live on. This statement is so simple and true, yet many artists ignore this basic concept, only willing to do the kind of art or subject matter they themselves like to do.

I understand. I have the same feeling about certain styles of painting, but I know the alternative is getting a full-time job to support myself, and doing so will pull me away from progressing as an artist.

I suggest that if you love doing your art and want to make a living on it, that you be willing to produce art that sells well to build a base income for that purpose. After you have a steady income coming in from your art, do the subject or kind of art you really want to do while maintaining your base income. If the work that you produce happens to be what sells really well, then all the better.

I've talked to many artists over the last few years who say they want to go full-time, but aren't willing to paint or make what sells because they find it boring. One lady said she only wants to paint nudes. Several artists I know who are very successful have told me they paint nudes, but only sell one a year. No one can survive on the sale of one or two originals a year!

Be willing to paint or make a variety of subjects. When you find a few that sell, make more of the same subject or type to keep the income flowing.

There are several markets that produce avenues of revenue for artists. For a complete list of the markets available I suggest a book called "Artist's & Graphic Designer's Market" Edited by Mary Cox - Writer's Digest Books - Cincinnati, Ohio.

For the sake of making things simple and less confusing, let's concentrate on two markets; the local market and the tourist market. The local market is people who live and work in your geographical area, and obviously, the tourist market is people who live elsewhere and are visiting your geographical area to see the sights or partake in local events. I have found that often the two , even though separate, do intertwine.

The local market is harder to break into , the tourist market is much easier to break into, By focusing on the tourist market you will also be exposing yourself to the local market as well. Inevitably you will be selling to both markets.

Tourism is Big Bucks

Many of the states in the U.S. recognize this and with the economic downturn of local industries they have turned their focus to increasing tourism to support local communities. There is no reason why you as an artist shouldn't make an income from the existing tourism industry your state has worked so hard to build with their advertising dollars.

Now it's true some states have more tourism than others. Positioning yourself and /or your art at a place (city or state) where your art can sell is a very important consideration. Many artists don't want to be in the hub of a busy place; they like being out in a secluded place where they can focus and be creative with out stress and interruption. Others choose to locate where tourism is high and they can be close to their venders and close to the subjects the tourists buy images of.

One key element in producing art that sells: "People buy what they experience."

It doesn't matter if you live out in the country or in the city. Find out why people visit your region, what they come to see and what they do while they are there. That is what you draw or paint and that is what you market to the tourists that visit your area.

I set out with a goal about three or four months after I went full-time - to paint local scenes, wild-life and events. Things people experience while visiting my local area. Within a few months I had a small collection of paintings and prints available to sell to the tourists passing through my town. Again and again people commented to each other "Oh, we were just there yesterday. I love this beach!"; "This painting of the moon over the palm trees reminds me of the other night - let's get it.." Some even said, "I like this one of the turtle, but will wait to get the print until after we see one."

"People buy what they experience" and they are looking for something they can take home to re-mind them of their trip or vacation. They are also looking for something they can buy as gifts for their family and friends back home. The fact that they are buying something made by a local artist makes it that much more desirable. After all, who wants to visit a place they've saved all year to visit and then buy a cheap trinket mass produced in China?

You as a local artist have a insight into your area. Portray that in your work. Painting local scenes is a great way to build a base income for your art business.

Each month I produced two to three more paint-ings and made prints to sell, each month my gross sales increased by several hundred dollars and then more than quadrupled at the height of the tourist season.

Review:

- Paint what people experience
- Place yourself and/or your art where tourists stop, shop and visit

Chapter Two
Reproducing Your Art in Small Print Form

No revolution of the past has ever done as much for the artist as the technical revolution has done for the artist of today.

It use to be much harder and more expensive to reproduce your art. Only the rich could afford to have reproductions made, or you had to be discovered by a publisher who was willing to front the cost. An artist who had low income could only make money on selling originals one at a time.

It wasn't that long ago that artists who thought they had a great seller would go to the expense of having lithograph prints made of their art only to discover it wasn't a great seller and they ended up with a $3,000 dollar box of prints under their bed that they can't sell.

As an artist in the digital age, the equipment is available and affordable for you to own yourself. Instead of spending thousands of dollars getting lithographic reproductions made of just one of your art images, you can now print your own art one at a time using professional printing equipment that you own.

Not only is the equipment available for making small prints, but there are more and more printing and publishing companies who will produce reproductions of your work in large formats for a low price one at a time. This kind of service for the artist has never been available before, and takes the gamble and expense out of getting your art career off the ground.

Reproducing your art makes it possible to sustain a monthly income that you can live on. I know if I had to depend on the sale of my original paintings alone, I wouldn't be working as a artist full-time yet. Some months I sell two or three originals and some months I don't sell any.

Copyrights

As an artist you hold the copyright and reproduction rights to your images. To retain the copyright you must simply place a copyright mark on the original with your name or signature and the year of creation.

When you sell an original painting, the customer now owns the painting, but does not own the copyrights and is prohibited by law from making reproductions of your original art. Even if you are commissioned to paint one that you deem saleable in print form, you hold the rights to reproduce it.

In this case however, I recommend out of courtesy that you let them know your intentions to reproduce the original and give them the option of paying extra to have you not make reproductions.

Most people who have commissioned me to paint scenes for them have had no problem with me making reproductions, but one individual insisted that he have the original and that it be the only one ever made and never reproduced. I explained that reproducing a piece of art is a major part of my art business, one image is worth several thousand dollars in sales over the next year, and I would have to charge him extra to agree not to make any reproductions. He agreed to pay the extra, I wrote a contract stating I still owned the copyrights, but that he had paid me not to exercise that copyright in any way shape of form. What you charge is up to you, but they should pay something extra for limiting your income over the next year.

I often remind clients I do commissions for of this: Having limited edition prints made of an image of art increases the value of the original because it gains notoriety in view of the art buying public.

Kinds of Art Buyers

There are many different kinds of art buyers, some want originals only, some want limited edition prints and for some a small print is just fine. They also have different budgets. Reproducing your images in different sizes and in different forms makes it possible to sell to art buyers in every budget range.

In an effort to make what I'm talking about less vague, here is a list of what I sell and the prices they sell for:

- 3"x4" refrigerator magnets = $5.00
- Pack of greeting cards (2) = $5.00
- 5"x7" Print (8x10 mat size) = $20.00
- 8"x10" Print (11x14 mat size) = $35.00
- 11"x14" Print (16x20 mat size) = $60.00
- 11"x14" Limited Edition Print (16x20 mat size)=$65.00
- 12"x16" Limited Edition Giclee canvas print = $367.00
- 16"x20" Limited Edition Giclee canvas print = $495.00
- 24"x30" Limited Edition Giclee canvas print = $895.00

Later on in this book I will get into the details of what equipment to get, materials and where to buy them and how to put together and package your art.

Digital Prints

There are many types of reproductions available, but I only use a couple. My small prints I call "Art Paper Prints." They are digital reproductions and are printed with an Epson Stylus Photo 2200 printer that uses archival inks that are pigment based rather than dye based. I use an Epson glossy photo paper and a Epson Heavy Matte Paper.

I also have Giclée prints made by a professional Giclée maker, they produce these for me on canvas and have several different kinds of art paper available to print on also.

About Giclée Prints

The name Giclée (jhee-clay) is French, and means to spray or to squirt. The Giclée process defined, is a means to digitally print on various substrates with archival inks at high quality. Giclées are produced using a high end ink jet printer where the resolution is such that the tone appears continuous to the viewer. In the Giclée process, a fine stream of ink - more than four million droplets per second - is sprayed onto archival art paper or canvas.

The beauty of the Giclée process is, that once the image is color corrected and archived, additional prints can be produced without up front cost. In other words, they can be printed on demand. This eliminates the need for artists to produce an entire edition all at once, saving money and time.

Laser Prints

Another way to reproduce your art, which is used by many watercolor artists who produce their originals in small sizes, is the laser color copy. Many artists use it and have told me they hold up really well to ultra violet light (UV).

If you are a watercolor artist and are on a small budget, this is a good way to get started until you can afford to move up to making digital prints of your art.

Photo Prints

Several artists I know today still use the photo process. Take 35mm shots of your work and get it developed. After choosing your best photo of it, take it back to the developer, have it cropped to size and have more photos made of it in various sizes (5x7, 8x10 & 11x14). Decide on what quantity of each size will get you the best price. Then mat them and sell them as photo reproductions of your art. This is a good shortcut for those starting out on a small budget.

Chapter Three
Getting Your Art Ready for Reproduction

I can't stress enough the importance of getting each and every piece of art ready for reproduction before you sell the original. Even if you have no intention of making prints right away, having your work in a reproducible format on file will help you in the future.

Transparency Option

Color transparencies are high quality and perfect for reproducing from, archiving, and are often the only acceptable form used by judges of art and art galleries who want to preview your art before they accept you for a showing.

Transparencies are the first step of a two step process. The second step is to produce a digital file of your image. This is done either by what is called a drum scan or done by a transparency scanner. Most companies that reproduce your art, do so by using digital data. The best way to find out who in your local area is doing transparencies and scans is to ask your local art store and other artists, or search for one on the web.

Getting the transparencies made and filing them as a archival record of your work is a good idea. Then, when you need them, they can be pulled out years later to be reproduced in any format.

The cost for having transparencies made can run anywhere from $35.00 to $75.00 for each piece of art. The drum scan or transparency scan will cost you anywhere between $25.00 to $50.00. The cost isn't much for the value they provide in multiple uses, but if your on a low budget, the expense can add up fast.

Low Budget Digital Option

Starting with a low budget myself, it didn't take me long to look for a less expensive way to make digital reproductions of my originals. I discovered in my search that I could make reproductions of my art in print form up to 11x17 in size and still have a good quality print by using a digital camera. I started paying a friend to shoot my art with his 3.2 mega pixel Nikon Digital Camera. He would charge me $15.00 per piece of art to shoot it and transfer it to a 100 megabyte zip disk.
I would then take it into a program called Photo-Shop®, click "Auto-Levels," crop it and I have a digital file that is ready to print.

After a few months of using this process, I purchased a Sony Cybershot 5.0 mega pixel digital camera ($985.00). Shooting your own art is the most cost effective way to start making reproductions in small print form (5x7's, 8x10's & 11x14's). On the other hand the disadvantage is that if you haven't had transparencies made of your art, when you are approached by a greeting card company, gallery, or want to submit your work to a magazine for a contest, your digital file may or may not be acceptable.

Professional Digital Scan Option

Some artists now are going digital all the way. With the new large format digital cameras and flatbed scanners available, many artists are skipping the transparency and just using professionally shot or scanned digital images. Having your art scanned directly rather than using transparencies will actually give you a better quality digital reproduction. I do this rather than have transparencies made.

The people who make my Giclées scan my original art, and I then have a high quality digital file that can easily make a reproduction the same size as the original painting. This saves lots of money because I don't need the transparency to make prints of my art. The disadvantage is that if I want to enter contests that require transparencies or slides, I can't enter. If you are using the digital process to make your prints and you can afford to have transparencies made also, do it.

One of the advantages of using a professional who is set up to scan art work, rather than shooting your art with your own digital camera is improved lighting. They are set up with a studio that has lighting made for reproducing art without getting reflection in the image. If you've ever tried shooting your own work with a camera, you know what kind of problems a glossy painted surface can give you. The other big advantage is that the digital files are much better than you can get with your digital camera.

Standard Print Sizes

One thing to consider when selling prints of your art is the size of your reproductions. When I first started out I chose my canvas size based on what I was in the mood to paint on. I soon discovered some odd sizes were difficult and expensive to buy mats and frames for. Your customers will be more likely to buy your art if it's easy to frame and they can buy the size frame they need at Wal-Mart or wherever they shop. If they have to go to the trouble of going to a frame shop to order a special size, you will lose a portion of your market for art sales. Choose canvas or paper sizes that scale down to or close to standard size prints used in photography (5x7, 8x10 & 11x14). To do this I started painting on sizes of canvas, from small to large; 8x10, 11x14, 16x20, 22x30 & 30x40. These sizes scale down to fit close enough that small adjustments can be made to make them fit the standard sizes of prints that I sell.

Chapter Four
Pricing Your Art Prints

Pricing your art reproductions, is pretty simple: Price them the same as other artists in your area are selling theirs for.

It doesn't matter if you are new to the art world and the other artists have already made a name for themselves. The price of a 11x14 Print, for instance, should be the same. The cost to produce them is about the same. In fact if the other artists are producing large quantities of prints, they are probably paying less than you. So don't mark yours down, and don' t think you are any less of an artist than the other guy or gal because you are new.

If someone likes an image they will pay the going rate. They won't choose a piece of art that is $2.00 cheaper over one they really like. Art buyers will buy art in their general budget range, and will buy one that speaks to them. Having prints marked with different prices only confuses them.

Price what the market will bear. Price the same as others in your local market. If the prices you see vary, then choose the average going price and mark yours the same. Matted, packaged and ready to frame prints in my area sell for:

- 8x10 mat size (with 5x7 prints) = $15.00 to $20.00
- 11x14 mat size (with 8x10 prints) = $30.00 to $35.00
- 16x20 mat size (with 11x14 prints) = $50.00 to $70.00

Double matted prints are usually a little more, that explains some of the price variance.

I have talked with several artists who are starting out and who sell their prints at half the price I sell my art prints for. I try to encourage them to make them the same price as mine, not for any selfish reason, but because I want to see them succeed. If you are going to sell your work, you should make a profit at it, and the money you make from it, you can use to buy more or better equipment. If you charge half the going rate, then you will forever struggle to make any money at it, and eventually you will give up. Value your art enough to price it so you make a profit and people will value your art enough to buy it.

When it comes to selling your art, think like a business man, not like an artist. Remember, you have to set the retail price of an art print based on what it will sell for in a consignment store. You still want to be able to make money on a print when you sell it wholesale to a store.

For example: A 8x10 mat size (5x7 print) sells retail for $20.00. You get 50% and the store gets 50%, so your wholesale price is $10.00. I figure, it costs me about $4.00 to put one together, so your profit if you sell it wholesale is only $6.00. But, when you sell a print yourself at the retail price of $20.00, your profit is $16.00.

If you sell a print that size for $10.00 retail, your profits are so small that you could never sell them wholesale and make any money on consignments.

Pricing your originals is a little different than pricing print reproductions. I have heard all kinds of theories on pricing original art, and been given conflicting advice from various people. The best advise I found was to start out low and raise the prices of your originals as they start selling well.

Eight months into my full-time art business I was selling my 16x20 original oil paintings for $200.00 each and was selling two a month. Then, nine months later, I sold the same size for $500.00 to $975.00 depending on how well they turn out and how much time I spent on them. (For more on pricing originals, see chapter 16).

One of my more popular images I painted is on a 16x20 canvas. I spent about 80 hours working on it, and was asking about $400.00 for it when I first finished it. Once I saw how well the prints sold during the first month, I decided the value of the original should be more and I marked it up to $800.00. As the demand continues to increase for the limited edition Giclée canvas prints and the more of them that are sold, the more the value of the original increases. This is true even if you have already sold the original, who ever owns it has a piece of art that is continually increasing in collection value. Having limited edition prints made of a image of art increases the value of the original because it gains notoriety in view of the art buying public.

If you calculate how much I make per hour ($800.00 divided by 80 = $10.00) you will see even at an asking price of $800.00, I'm only making $10.00 per hour on the original. That's not very much, but let me share with you a belief that has brought me a lot of success. If I spend the time to put in extra details that make my paintings sharper, clearer and more dynamic, then my re-productions will be sharper clearer and more dynamic. I may not make much per hour on my originals, but my prints will sell better and I can sell prints long after the original is sold.

For example; My 16x20 oil painting of the "Place of Refuge" I had priced at $800.00. But because I did an incredible job painting it, people are drawn to it and express their appreciation as they walk by and see the image of it at my place of business. In the first two months after its creation, I made $695.00 in print sales and $1,200.00 in Giclée canvas print sales on that image alone. Each month that goes by, I sell more of that image. I eventually did sell the original, but it took almost a year before a buyer came along that was willing to pay the asking price.

The return on my investment of time goes beyond the original to the reproductions, creating a residual income for me in the long run. The extra time I've invested comes back to me, but the greatest value is in the impression it makes on people, making my exposure a positive one as it builds my art career.

Some artists feel their original work, even though they are just beginning their art career, is worth thousands of dollars. They choose to keep the price they demand for the original at their asking price and sell limited edition prints of it. I know of a few who do this and get their asking price. Their work is exceptional and every gallery that sees it wants to carry it.

If this is you, I suggest your time is better spent hand highlighting Giclée prints, painting originals and filling the demands of the galleries who want your work. If you want or need extra income while doing that, there is always a market for your art in the small print form that I'm writing about in this book.

Some artists who have gained momentum in their art careers save their originals for their retirement. Having seen the value of their art and its popularity rise, they set some or all of them aside, knowing when they retire they can sell them for five or ten times their original value. Keep this in mind when you get to a place in your career where you can afford to do the same.

Chapter Five
Working as a Street Artist?

The name of the game for any artist is "exposure." If you want to put yourself and your art on the fast track to making a living as an artist, get on the street in a busy public place.

Working as a street artist for me has been not only financially beneficial, but from it I've been commissioned to paint several originals, been invited to join galleries, been asked to sell wholesale to gift shops and met people from all over the world who like and collect my art.

There's something dynamic that happens when people see you working/painting on the street. It creates an ambiance. People like seeing artists being creative and will stop to see what you are doing. You can use this dynamic to your advantage by having a small display of prints with you to sell.

Deciding whether or not working as a street artist is for you is a personal choice. Before you decide it's not for you or that you can't do it because you get nervous when people watch you, let me say that it's just like anything else in life. We get nervous doing new and different things at first, but after a while it becomes second nature and we just do it without thinking. If you are nervous or new to working in front of people, here is a way to ease into it a little at a time. Start drawing or painting at a location like a public park. Be near a sidewalk or path where when people walk by, they can casually look over your shoulder to see what you are doing. More times than not, you'll get comments about your work. I usually just look at them, smile, say thank you and return to my work.

Finding a Location

The first thing your going to need to work as a street artist is a location. Finding the right location to work and sell your art can make a big difference in your art sales and ultimately the life or death of your art business.

The first thing to find out is when the tourist season starts and when does it end in your area. With this in consideration, find out where the tourist "hot spot" is.

Then spend some time observing the tourists. This can take several days, a week or more. You are looking for information:

- Where is the most walk-by traffic?

- What time of day is the best time to be on the street selling? This is generally when you have the most foot traffic.
- What is the walk-by traffic like at night and is it the same place as during the day?
- What days of the week have more tourists than other days?
- What areas are well lighted at night or has an electrical outlet so I can bring my own lighting.

When I first started, I did this and decided I wanted a studio location, but because the rents where I needed to be were $4,000.00-$10,000.00 per month, I couldn't afford to rent a small studio/gallery location. I ended up renting a place that was in a hallway just off the main drag of the tourist flow. The rent was $400.00 per month plus utilities, but being out of the tourist flow by only 40 feet proved fatal to my art business. I only got passer-by traffic from people looking for the restrooms, and I only made enough to pay the rent and utilities.

I was invited by a guy who managed a time-share store front on the main drag to sit and paint in his front window. He wanted me to paint, display and sell my art to draw attention to his store so people would come in to look. I closed my shop and moved in.

It was at this point that I began to realize that working as a street artist had value, not only to me but to others, making it a marketable commodity. My sales more than tripled the first month! The dynamic of working in the open in front of people was working for me and for the store owner also.

Working as a Draw

This dynamic can work for you too, and you can use it to get yourself a great location! Most business men and women are looking for something to make their store stand out from the others, they are usually restricted from having more signage by city codes and ordinances. Most will usually be willing to at least try letting you have a small 4x5 or 8x5 foot area out front as long as what you are selling compliments them and doesn't compete with what they are selling inside. That is assuming they have the room for you to be out there.

You can try going from location to location talking to managers and store owners, but I recommend if you are painting local scenes that you simply ask if you can sit out front and paint to capture a local scene across or down the street. Being there to paint and not sell at first will give the store operator a chance to see first hand what kind of attention you draw just by being there. Go back several times to finish the painting if possible, then do the same at several other locations.

One place where I painted invited me to return and paint any time I wanted. Later, after I gave up my studio, I asked if I could paint there again a few days a week and sell prints while I was there. They agreed, and I painted there four days a week for eight months until I moved on to another location. They wanted me there more than four days a week because my being there drew attention and brought them more business than when I wasn't there. All the colors of the paintings brightens up the sidewalk, people stop to look at them and then look up to see what store is there, some go in and some come back later and go in.

At another place I painted in front of, I spoke with the property manager about renting a place on the sidewalk in the plaza. The manager showed me a grassy spot in front of a coffee shop, we spoke with the owner and he was okay with the idea of me painting outside. I asked how much for the space, and the property manager said lets just try it out and I will let you know. Three months later I asked again and she said the property owner liked having an artist out there and felt it added value to the plaza. She said, keep going like you are going (rent free) but to tell anyone who asked that I was renting the space.

The coffee shop owner loved having me outside painting and let me plug in my electrical cord for my lights at night. To show my gratitude, I gave him a free large print every couple of months as payment for the electricity I used.

At another location, I approached the property manager about setting up and painting in front of his plaza. I explained that I was a street artist and was looking for a location to paint and sell my art, I also explained how I work as a draw for other stores that I sit in front of. I was offered the spot at that location on a regular basis for 10% of my sales. I accepted, how could I lose? A great location and I only have to pay rent if I sell some art. If I got rained out or was sick and not able to go to work, I didn't have to pay rent for the space.

How you negotiate how much time, what times and rent is between you and the owner of the store. I've worked with several different places and each one was different. One of the places where I painted wasn't allowed to sub-rent, and considered the attention I drew to his store payment enough. Out of gratitude I started placing small advertisements on the backs of my prints that said "Sponsored by......" with his company logo on it.

When working as a draw for someone else, your priority is to draw attention by working on your art, verbally promote the store and be helpful any way you can while working and selling your art. As long as you have a good attitude and are a asset to the store you sit in front of, you will always be welcomed back. I even swept and wiped tables when I saw it needed to be done.

Working Advertisement

Another value you have to offer as a street artist is advertisement. That's right! You're sitting with your back to a crowd who is looking over your shoulder at what you are working on. Your back is a great spot for a promotional advertisement and you can sell or trade that advertising space for cash or something you use everyday that you pay cash out for. I traded mine for coffee, and the coffee company provided the shirts with their logo and ad. So, while I was working on the street, I got free coffee all day long!

One thing that I've noticed in finding a location is that people gather for food, coffee, ice cream and shave ice, especially at night after dinner. Getting a well lighted location near or at an establishment that serves any of these items is good. Another thing I noticed, depending on the location, is that sales after dinner are often as good as the sales I've made all day long. In my area this has more to do with the fact that people are out at the beach and exploring during the day and then they go out to dinner and then shop in the cool of the evening.

Here are a few photos of a place I painted in front of a few years ago. Compare how it looks with me set up out front to how it looks without me there.

Here: Not set up.

Here: I'm set up.

People walk across the street just to see my art - it's a draw that works!

Another location. Before I built a display table to get the prints off the ground.

Logistics

One of the things you'll have to deal with as a street artist is setting up and breaking down your area. Often, there is no space to store your display racks, umbrellas and artwork. You will have to bring all these things with you and take them home when you leave. Most of the locations I've had over the years were like that, and a few had places out of the way that I could use to lock my display racks and umbrellas up.

I don't take more with me than I can carry in my car, and to do that I've had to learn to pack the car very well. For my art prints, I use blue plastic boxes with lids (storage bins). For my displays, when I didn't have a place to store them, I use to tie them to the roof of the car.

To get the art prints and my displays to and from the car in one trip, I use a hand truck with a handle that is adjustable (It has to fit in the car also).

On the following page you will find photos of my art prints packed on the cart and my display stuff locked up behind a fence.

Here is a photo of my display set up:

Having a place to store your display equipment makes it a lot easier and the blue storage boxes have enough room for extra prints, so I have several back-up prints with me to restock when I sell one.

Recording Sales

I keep a note book with me that has record sheets in it for recording sales. The date, art print title, size, type of item (print, magnet, card, T-shirt, etc.), day of the week, pay type (CC for credit card, TC for travelers check and cash), and the amount the item was sold for are recorded.

Recording sales is important for several reasons:
1. Records of which images and what sizes sold is good information to have. You can track the best sellers and list the top ten when choosing which prints to put in consignment stores.
2. You have a list of prints sold that day to refer to later that night when you go home and restock inventory.
3. Good records makes filing taxes easy at tax time.

On the next page is a photo of my record sheet.

Daily Retail Sales Record Sheet:

Date	Art Title:	Size:	Type:	Day:	Pay Type	Amount:

Breaking into the Art World - by Marshall White

I have provided a template of this record sheet on my web site that you can download for free. www.SuccessfulArtist.com/templates.htm

Art Shows

Another option to working as a street artist is art shows, or you could do both. There are usually arts and craft shows and art exhibits at local events and festivals. Sometimes they are worth the entry fee to get in and other times they aren't. I've heard from other artists I know that they do really well at some of them. You have to try them out and see which ones work best for you. Either way it's good exposure for you and your art and may lead to some new clients and good contacts.

A call for entries is usually posted in the newspaper a few months before the event. The best way to find out about art and craft shows in your area is to ask other artists. They can usually tell you which ones are worth entering.

Review:
- When is tourist season?
- Where are the tourists "hot spots"?
- When are the best days and times?
- Get a place to paint and sell, working as a draw
- Logistics
- Recording sales
- Art shows

Chapter Six
Selling Your Art

Let me first state that selling anything is an art in itself. I've never considered myself a salesman or thought that I had a gift for sales. In fact just the opposite is true, I'm an artist first and selling just happens to be one small part of making a living as an artist.

I don't pretend to know a lot about sales and continue to learn as I go. The best book I've read on the subject is: "Retail selling made easy" by Ron Martin (September, 1996. Booklines Hawaii Ltd). I recommend reading it. It's informative and will save you lost sales commonly made by trial and error.

Fortunately for us as artists, selling art isn't as hard as selling other things. People will either like an image or they won't. If they like it and they have the money, they will buy it. Your art will pretty much sell itself once you put it on display.

Having said that, here are a few pointers to help you sell more than your work will sell on its own:

Smile - That's right! Smile and say "hi." Remember, you are not only selling your art, you are selling yourself. Smiling is an international language that makes you approachable, and when people feel they can approach you, they are more likely to.

Demonstrate - An artist friend of mine gave me this advise and I found it to be true. "If you're not painting - you're not selling!" Drawing or painting while on location to sell generates interest and excitement. When people see work in progress and like what they see, they are more likely to buy. This has worked for other artists working on the street, in the studios, and in galleries. It has also worked for me. I know one artist who paints in a gallery. Not only did the overall gallery sales increase while he was there painting, but his own sales at the gallery increased as well.

One important thing to remember is not to get so lost in work that potential customers are ignored. Say "hi," welcome them to ask questions, and continue to work. Be attentive to them, watch for them to be ready to buy.

Additionally, be aware that when selling art that there are several different kinds of buyers. Some don't want to be bothered, they just want to focus on how each image makes them feel. Others want information before they buy. They want conversation with you, the artist, your history, your training, etc. Talking with them often makes the difference from a "no sale" to a "sale."

Eye contact - Smile, look them in the eye, say "hi," and be enthusiastic! Smiling says you are friendly, pupil to pupil contact says you are trustworthy, and greeting them opens the door for conversation and questions they might have. Enthusiasm, is simply contagious. If they catch it, they may well get enthused about you and your art. Being enthusiastic is important, if you look tired and lazy, depressed or ho-hum, sales will be lost. People usually don't want to buy if they perceive that you don't care that they are at your booth and could care less about selling.

Rest - Get lots of it! It's hard to be creative when you are tired and it's also hard to be enthusiastic . If you are tired or in a bad mood, push yourself to be enthusiastic, put on your "promotion face" and do your best.

Don't complain! - Ever! About anything! Especially never say anything negative about another artist. Don't complain or gossip in front of customers. Negative attitudes and negative talk always backfire.

Be clean & dress clean - Always be clean as possible and wear clean clothes. Don't under dress or over dress while selling. If you are painting while selling, always look fresh and clean, wearing your best work clothes.

Hooks

Having a hook is one way to increase sales. The longer you can get a potential customer to stand in front of your booth and look, the better chance you have of making a sale.

I stumbled onto this hook by accident; I painted a couple of pictures with hidden words in them. As it turns out, having people look for the hidden words has become one of my better sales tools. When someone stops to look I say "hi," pause and let them look. If they look like they are about to walk away, I ask them if they saw the paintings with the hidden words. I show them the first one and tell them what the word is and let them discover it. I provide hints if needed. Then I show them the second one. If they enjoy looking for the words, I ask them if they would like to see the other paintings with the hidden things. Sometimes they buy one, sometimes they tell others in town about my art with the hidden words, either way my art business benefits.

I also use this when someone is looking at my art and I see others walking by behind them; I ask the person in front of me, "Did you see this one? It has the word Hawaii hidden in it." Usually the people walking by stop in their tracks. Curious, they join in and I suddenly have an audience crowding around me looking for the hidden words and now looking at my art instead of just walking by.

There are many different things you can do without interrupting the flow of your art. Some artists hide insects, small animals, birds or whatever their favorite thing is. When people find out you hide things in your art, they usually rise to the challenge of finding them.

Add-on Sales

Every sales person that is good at sales knows about "add-ons." Add-ons are the attempt to get a person to buy more than they came in for. I'm not aggressive, so I use a subtle approach. Many people who stop by my booth ask about getting a discount, or ask if they can buy one and get one free. If I did that for every one who asks me, I'd be a starving artist - not a successful one.

So, here is something I do to encourage people to buy more art prints: buy four and get the fifth one free. Many people who already have two or three prints in their hands will go for it, and I have a sign on my display that says, "Buy 4 and get the 5th one FREE (same size or smaller)." If they buy four instead of two, I can afford to give one away. If they decide not to buy at all because I won't give them what they want, I tell them, "I'm sorry, but I have my art prints in several stores here in town and if I under-cut them, they won't carry my art anymore." If they still don't buy because I don't give them what they want, I let them pass. I have a reputation to maintain and kids at home to feed, I can't give away my profits.

I make the same offer to the consignment retailers, so I'm not cheating on them. I've told them to offer the same and I'll split the price of the fifth one with them. So that both the store and I benefit from it.

Convenience Marketing

Most of the people I sell to are tourists and getting art prints home without damaging them is a big concern. Offering to ship the prints they purchase is a plus for you. Sometimes they won't buy anything just because they don't want to carry it home. I offer shipping and have a sign that says so. I don't make money on the shipping, I just do it to encourage customers to buy my art. I charge from small sizes to large; $6.00, $10.00 and $18.00.

On a large 16x20 frame size print, the shipping from Hawaii to the U.S. Mainland is about $11.00, the box is about $5.00 and the bubble wrap is a few bucks.

To encourage add-ons; I offer FREE shipping with a $100.00 or more purchase of my art prints. It works! Instead of just buying one print and paying shipping for it, they buy more just to get the free shipping.

I use to ship the next day after the purchase was made, but since I'm not making money for standing in line at the Post Office, I now tell customers that I ship every Friday. I do all my shipping at once and the customer almost always understands.

Methods of Receiving Payment

When I first started selling my art on the street as a street artist, I only accepted cash, travelers checks and local checks (with photo ID). I wasn't set up to receive credit cards for at least a year. It proved to be a big hassle for customers as they would have to walk down the street to find a cash machine. Of course, I told them exactly where they could find one, but often they would never return to purchase my art.

Depending on who you use, a credit card machine can cost you around $35.00 to $50.00 per month. When I realized I was losing more than that every week in lost sales, I figured it would be cheaper to have one than not to have one.

As it turns out, having one was better than I originally thought. I wasn't losing sales and not only did the convenience make customers happy, sometimes they would spend more than they would have if they had used cash.

You can ask other retailers who they use for their credit card processing. There are different options, so shop around. I use Pacific Card Services out of Honolulu, Hawaii. You might consider using them, they have been very helpful and treated me well, and they already work with artists and crafters all over the United States. Their phone number is: (808)-306-6611, ask for "Dean," and be sure to tell him Marshall White sent you.

The machine I have for receiving credit cards is the Verifone Tranz 420. It is an older machine and there may be newer ones, but it works like this: it has a rechargeable battery so you can take it on location where there is no power available. If a phone line is available, you can see if customers credit cards are valid right away when the purchase is being made. I don't have a phone line, so I receive their card, print out the receipt and have the customer sign it.

The information is stored to "batch." At the end of the day when I get home, I plug the machine into a phone line and submit my batch report. At this point I find out if the customers card is good or not. It's risky for me to do it this way, but my street locations aren't set up for phone lines so I'm stuck taking the risk. I've been pretty lucky so far and only lost a few sales each year from credit cards that were declined.

There are machines you can get that are wireless and use a cellular connection to authorize cards on the spot, but if you live in a remote location like I do where the service isn't offered, you will have to consider for yourself if taking the risk is worth it.

Review:
- Smile and greet
- Demonstrate
- Converse with people
- Look them in the eye
- Be enthusiastic
- Get lots of rest
- Don't complain or gossip
- Good hygiene & dress well
- Hooks
- Add-on sales
- Convenience marketing
- Make purchasing your art convenient

Chapter Seven
Keys to a Successful Art Business

Here are several keys to success, that are not specific to the art business, but are common key elements to any successful business.

- Be consistent
- Be prompt
- Be positive
- Provide a quality product at a fair price
- Have goals
- Good presentation
- Do one thing each day to advance your career/ to reach your goals

Be consistent - If you have a location or studio/gallery, it's important to be consistent. Be open on the days you are to be open and be there the hours you commit to be there. Be consistent at providing quality work, a good presentation, a positive attitude and a professional handling of business from start to finish.

Be Prompt - Always be on time to appointments. If you have a location, always be on time. Return phone calls and messages as soon as possible. Fill orders quickly and accurately. Make sure when galleries and gift shops place an order for more of your art to provide it right away.

Be Positive - Let your thoughts and your speech dwell on the good things in your life. Be a "The glass is half full" kind of person, not a "The glass if half empty" kind of person.

Everyone who is living has challenges and obstacles to overcome in their life. Choose to be thankful for the good things in life and let your focus be on them. Customers and potential clients can spot and will avoid negative people - so *be positive.*

Provide Quality Products at a Fair Price - Whatever you do, do it well. Always provide your customers with your best materials, never try to sell damaged or sub-standard merchandise.

Have Goals - Having a goal will give your life and business direction, helping you to focus day to day to reach that goal. Without a goal, you will waste time, energy and money wandering aimlessly. Setting a goal is easy, choose one main objective. It can be what you want to do, what you want to be or how much you want to make, etc.

For me, my goal is to make a living as an artist, to do what I enjoy and make enough money to live on doing it.

Once you know your main goal, break it down into smaller goals. Ask this question; What do I have to do to make my main goal happen?

Make a list of the things you need to do. Then if needed, write out what you need to do to accomplish the smaller goals. Working each day on something on the list will bring you closer to your main objective.

Before I make large purchases for my business or my home, I always ask myself; "Will this bring me closer to my goals, or will it take me further away?"

Have a Good Presentation - Having a good presentation includes; Presenting yourself clean, nicely dressed and polite. It also includes the presentation of your art. (See chapter fourteen for more on this).

Do one thing each day to advance your career/ to reach your goals - Part of reaching your goals is making contacts with buyers. Try to make at least one new contact each day to let them know about your art, in person, by phone, or over the internet.

- Make a new contact
- or, Provide a new contact or existing contact with promotional material
- Work on, or finish an objective that gets you closer to your goal

Being an artist and running your own business of selling your art is a lot of work. Each day I juggle what needs to be done for the business side, the art side and my family life (personal time). Getting the right balance isn't easy, but it can be done.

What is Success?

How can you ever reach success if you can't define it?

It's not enough to say I want to be successful and only have a vague idea of what success is. You must define for yourself what success is, and you should write it down. Don't define it by any one else's standards. Write out your own definition of success, and under it make a list of criteria you must meet or exceed to be considered successful.

For example:

I define success as simply; "Doing what I love and making a living at it."

- Painting and making my art
- Paying all the bills
- Having food, clothing and a roof over my head
- At least one car
- Waking up each morning excited to be alive
- Meeting my commitments

I work hard to meet all of these elements I define as part of being successful. When any one of these elements starts lacking in my life, I work hard and do what I can to meet it. Part of paying all the bills is also trying to keep my overhead low and not adding more bills to the pile to be paid. Stay out of debt, or at least don't get any deeper into it.

What ever you do - KEEP IT SIMPLE. There's no good that comes out of defining success as something you don't believe you will ever reach in your lifetime.

Review:

- Be consistent
- Be prompt
- Be positive
- Provide a quality product at a fair price
- Have goals
- Good presentation
- Do one thing each day to advance your career/ to reach your goals
- Define Success

Chapter Eight
Consignments

Whether you choose to be a street artist or not, you're going to want to have consignments. Placing your art up for sale in different locations not only increases your income, but it also increases your exposure as an artist. The more people see your work in different locations the more popular you appear in the eyes of the viewing public.

Stores, gift shops and artists galleries are looking for products they can sell and make a profit on. Approach them about carrying and selling you art prints. You can usually tell which ones would consider selling your style of art by looking at what they currently sell, but don't let that stop you from approaching them with your art. Let them make the final decision, you never know if what you have to offer is just what they've been looking for.

As an artist, you are in control of your art career, you paint or draw to sell well. You also want to be strategic in choosing places that will carry and sell your art. There is an up-front investment on your part when you agree to let a store carry and sell your work on consignment. It's important that your consignments be great locations on the main street where walk by traffic is high, or at locations where tourists frequently stop.

Remember, you want to make lots of sales so you can continue to produce your art. Choosing to place your art in a store or gallery off the beaten path where few people ever visit will be more of a disadvantage to you than an advantage.

Once you've identified "hot spots" where people often visit and shop, choose the stores, shops & galleries you want to approach. Approach them with this in mind: Find out if they buy and then sell instead of consign. Having a store or shop buy from you at wholesale is better than one that will consign at wholesale, it's a lot less work for you. Some smaller shops may pay when you deliver, most pay in thirty days.

Second, if they will sell your work on consignment, what percentage are they accustomed to getting? 40/60? 50/50? If they are used to 40% to the store and 60% to the artist and are willing to do the same with you, then write up a consignment agreement reflecting this percentage.

Most stores and shops I've talked to want 50/50, and want you to agree to having the retail price of your art the same everywhere else it sells, including your own retail sales. The customer should always pay the same price for the same size art print no matter who he/she buys it from.

This means if you are selling a 11x14 mat sized print for $35.00 retail, their wholesale cost is $17.50. As long as your retail price is the same across the board, you can still have different wholesale prices. In other words, it's okay to have an agreement with one store for 40/60% and an agreement with another for 50/50% as long as the retail price is the same in both stores. The fact that one is getting a better wholesale price than the other is privileged information and a matter of negotiation. You may have good reason why one gets a better deal than another, for example: Better locations that sell more of your work may deserve a bigger cut.

When you know the "hot" locations, you can use them to your advantage. If you want the location and know your art would sell well there, offer them 50/50% up front. But, if someone who has a location approaches you and wants to carry your art on consignment, and you know it's not a "hot" spot, offer them 40/60%. You are making the initial investment to stock their store and if it's not a prime location, you are therefore taking a risk. This gives you leverage to negotiate for the percentage you want - 40/60%.

Galleries vary in the kind of work they display, some won't carry small prints and other will only carry prints if they sell originals. Most galleries, if they want your work, will not accept anything less than 60/40 (60% to the gallery and 40% to the artist). Some higher end galleries want an even higher percentage. I have had, however, artist owned galleries who carry other artists work offer me 60%.

Look at it this way when you are dealing with higher end galleries; You get 40%, the gallery gets 40% and the professional salesperson gets a 20% sales commission (usually). A good sales person is worth their weight in gold! Instead of splitting the sales persons commission with the gallery, (where you would pay half and the gallery would pay half,) it's better to let the gallery take care of the whole thing. As an artist, you have enough to deal with without having to file taxes for paying a salespersons commissions all year long. Let the gallery take care of the whole thing, give them 60% and they can have the employee headaches and all the tax problems that go along with it.

When approaching stores, shops and galleries, it's important to be professional, even when they decide your work is not what they want to carry. Be kind and courteous to the end. Don't burn any bridges by acting like you're dejected. You've made a new contact who still may carry your work later on after your work has progressed.

The Approach

When making your approach, always be prepared. Take your business card, portfolio and a sample of one of your prints (packaged and ready to sell, so that they can see what the product looks like). It's also a good idea to give them a flier print out on 8 1/2x11 paper showing samples of your best sellers and contact information. That way if the buyer isn't there, they can see your work later.

Once they've agreed to carry your art, have them select the images they want to carry and sizes they want of each image. Having a list of your best sellers often helps them make the best business decision. After all, it doesn't do you any good if they select an image that rarely sells.

Give them a date you will return to stock their store with your art. Then go home and write out a "Consignment Agreement" based on your negotiations.

When stocking someone's store with your art, it's often expected that you will provide display bins for your art. This is to your advantage. You keep some control on how your art is presented to the public. Presentation Matters!

Consignment Agreement for Shops

Writing a basic consignment agreement is easy. Many artists use agreements, also called "contracts" when dealing with galleries and shops. Although, there are still a few out there who still prefer a verbal agreement and a handshake.

I recommend writing agreements, even if they are simple, to avoid future misunderstandings. You are entering into a business relationship with the gallery or shop. Having a basic agreement not only protects your interest, it also protects theirs. Having a "contract" shows you are professional and serious about business with them.

Here is a sample of a basic consignment agreement I use with shops.

Basic Consignment Agreement

I (*artist name*) agree to provide (*owner name*) of (*business name*), located in (*city and state*) with selected small print reproductions of my art at wholesale prices as follows: 50% to the artist/ 50% to the store.

8x10 prints: wholesale price =$10.00, suggested retail price =$20.00
11x14 prints: wholesale price =$17.50, suggested retail price =$35.00
16x20 prints: wholesale price =$30.00, suggested retail price =$60.00
16x20 Limited Edition prints: wholesale price =$32.50, suggested retail price =$65.00

I also agree not to sell or have any of my art reproductions sold by other stores located in the same shopping complex, and further agree to only sell prints at the same suggested retail price stated above.

The consignee agrees to display and sell selected art prints at the prices noted above and will pay (*artist name*) the agreed upon amount (even if the prints are stolen) at the end of each month when inventory is counted and restocked.

The consignee also agrees to return any displays provided by (*artist name*) for his/her art to (*artist name*) at the termination of this contract. (Does not include displays that have been purchased).

Displays (if provided for free) by (*artist name*) are for the sole purpose for the display of art by (*artist name*).

By signing this contract you agree with terms stated above.

Signature:_____
Date:_____

Signature:_____
Date:_____

Thank you,(*store owners name*), for carrying my art in your store. I look forward to a long, happy and profitable business relationship.

Best Regards,

(*artist name*)

———·———·———

Keep in mind I'm not a lawyer; nor do I claim that any basic agreement of contract that I write will stand up in a court of law. If you are wanting a legal document, I suggest you have one written up by a lawyer.

———·———·———

Note: Suggested retail prices are just that. You can't force a store to sell them at the exact same price, some will want to sell lower and some will sell higher. But, most stores will agree to sell them at the suggested retail price. They don't want the competition down the street selling them for less, so they are usually comforted to find out they sell the same everywhere they are available.

Recap:

1. State a title - "Basic Consignment Agreement" or "Consignment Contract." I prefer "agreement." Some people have a problem with the word "contract."

2. State who the agreement is between - You and the other person or shop.

3. Product information - State what products they will carry on consignment. Sizes and both wholesale and suggested retail prices. (%)

4. Price agreement - State that you, as the artist and the supplier, agree to sell at the same retail prices and never lower.

5. Location agreement - State that you agree not to sell wholesale or retail to any other shops within the same shopping plaza.

6. Theft protection - State that the shop (Name of Shop) is responsible for the products on consignment and must pay you, the artist the agreed wholesale price for the product even if the product is stolen.

7. Displays - If you provide displays for your art, make sure it's in the contract that you own them and that they should be returned to you if they stop carrying your art. Also state that the displays are for your art only. It's annoying to go into a store that carries your art on consignment and find someone else's art in your display, in front of your art.

8. Signature - Provide a place for both parties to sign and date the agreement.

(Make two copies to be signed, one for each party.)

Submit the agreement with the delivery and ask them to review it. Ask if it's satisfactory to them. If not, ask them if there is anything else you can add to the agreement to make it satisfactory.

Most shops realize this agreement protects them more than you and will sign it. If a shop refuses any agreement, you should be cautious and use your best judgment to decide if you want them to carry your product. I would ask around to see what kind of reputation they have in town with other artists.

Keeping Track of Consignments

Each month on the last day of the month I visit the stores and galleries that sell my art prints on consignment and check their stock to see how many prints they sold. I keep track of which ones they carry by title of the work of art. I check off each one that is in the display, the ones that aren't checked off have been sold. I then submit a bill for the amount sold and let them know I will return in a few days to restock the display.

Some of the stores and galleries I have agreements with are very organized and know exactly what they have sold, they prefer to send me a check for what has been sold along with a statement showing the title of the work and the size that was sold. For them, I simply deliver or mail them the prints for restock based on the information they have provided me.

Other stores I have agreements with are not so organized. They have no idea how many art prints they have sold and what sizes they were. For them, I check the stock myself every month against the record sheet I keep for their account.

Either way I keep a record of prints they carry and which ones they sold from month to month. I keep a copy for myself and give them a copy to keep in their records.

I have had several stores tell me that the way I keep track of my art prints is the best they've ever seen. One store owner said she works with more than 25 artists and none of them has a system that is as organized or as easy to understand.

I created the template for this system in Corel-Draw®. If you have CorelDraw®, you can download this template from my website: http://www.SuccessfulArtist.com/templates.htm

On the following page is a photo of what the record sheet looks like.

ARTIST NAME
Artist Address and Phone Number

FOR: Store Name   DATE: 1-15-2005   CONSIGNMENT [x]   PURCHASE [ ]

■ Current print stock
▨ New prints added to stock
▨ Sold prints
▨ Prints pulled from stock

-	SIZE	TITLE / DESCRIPTION	WHOLESALE	SOLD	PAID
	8x10	Koi Pond	$10.00		
	8x10	Koi Pond	$10.00		
	8x10	Honu at Mahai'ula Bay	$10.00		
	8x10	Find Kai	$10.00		
	11x14	Koi Pond	$17.50		
	11x14	Koi Pond	$17.50		
	11x14	Honu at Mahai'ula Bay	$17.50		
	16x20	Koi Pond	$32.50		
	16x20	Tropical Sunset	$32.50		
	16x20	Honu at Mahai'ula Bay	$32.50		
	Sold in December:				
	8x10	Koi Pond	$10.00		
	11x14	Koi Pond	$17.50		
	16x20	Tropical Sunset	$32.50		

The consignment inventory record sheet is color-coded and has a reference to what the colors mean. To see this in color, please view online at: http://www.SuccessfulArtist.com/templates.htm

If a customer carries five prints of the same image and they are all the same size for example, each print is shown on its own line. This helps to eliminate confusion when checking stock each month.

At the bottom of the page I make a note in red of which prints were sold and what size they were.

This system works really well and the colors make it less confusing because you can see which ones are new prints added and which ones have been pulled from stock at the time of restock.

When checking my stock, I always put a checkmark next to the print title if it is in the display, then the ones that aren't checked are sold. I put a check in the "Sold" column if they are not in stock.

Later I check the "Paid" column when the bill is paid and then place the paperwork back in its file for that account.

When I deliver the restock, I also provide an updated inventory sheet showing the date of restock and note the month. One copy for me and my files and one for the store.

Always have someone at the store check your stock in with you. Show them the sheet and have them check the prints with you to make sure they are all there. This is a security measure and will save you lots of hassles should some prints come up missing during the month.

Galleries

Most galleries will only carry your originals and Giclée prints. They usually already have a standard contract for you to sign, stating their expectations and rules you must agree to in order to be in their gallery. They are usually much more restrictive and commonly insist that no other sales be made, and that no other gallery carry your art within a 30 mile radius of their gallery.

For a better understanding of how galleries work and what you can expect when working with galleries I'll refer you to a book by Caroll Michels, Titled "How to Survive and Prosper as an Artist." (Published by: Henry Holt and Company, Inc.).

My book is more specific to what I do, her book covers a wide variety of art forms and is a "must have" for any new artist starting out in the art world.

My personal experience of working with galleries is limited (remember, as I write this book I'm still new to the art world). What I have learned from other artists I have talked to is that submitting your art to galleries by sending slides is expensive and is pretty ineffective. They (other more experienced artists) said it's better to mail fliers with ıples of your work. It's also easier to get into a gallery if another artist recommends you to the gallery.

Co-Op Galleries

Co-op galleries are galleries that are operated by the members of the gallery. All of the members are artists who display their art and take turns running and operating the gallery. Co-ops vary in the types of art they sell. They also vary in character or personality. Most, are usually operated by the artists and usually give the artist 75% and keep 25% for the gallery operating expenses.

For an artist just getting started, co-ops are a great way to get some exposure and at the same time learn a few things about operating a gallery, selling art and a little about the business end of art.

Most co-op members are very helpful and want to see you succeed as an artist, as well as themselves. The better each member becomes the better the gallery as a whole will do. Many co-op galleries have limited wall and floor space. Therefore, your membership can depend on several differing factors.

1. Do they have any openings?
2. Does your art compliment the other pieces in the gallery?
3. Are they looking for work in your medium?

It may be that you will have to wait until the right opportunity arises to join. Don't let that discourage you. Apply and check back each month to see if there are any openings.

Licensing

As you progress in your art and have a body of work (20-50 images), you might want to consider submitting your work to publishing companies. They pay royalties to artist for the use of their art. Once you find one that is interested in one of your images, they will send you a licensing contract to sign for the limited use of that image.

Depending on what kind of publishing they do, the contract could state the intended use of the image, how many years the license is for and what percent you as the artist will receive of the net after expenses. Publishing companies are usually very good at doing what they do. They know by experience what images will sell well in the various formats they publish in.

If your work happens to be the kind of work that publishing companies like and want, you may do very well and make lots of money on licensing your images alone.

Some of the more common uses for art images are:
- T-shirts
- Postcards
- Greeting cards

- Calendars
- Posters & prints
- Tiles
- Plates
- Coffee mugs
- Book covers, etc.

Chapter Nine
Art and the Internet

Ah, the internet, the new frontier. Like a modern day gold rush, many artists, including myself, rushed into the new global market place. Investing hundreds and even thousands to stake our claim on this new cyber-gold. Thousands, even millions would be buying our art as soon as we got our dot com set up with credit card processing online.

As it turned out many dot coms went bankrupt and the real cash was made by cyber leasing companies and web site builders who cashed in on cyber-gold miners on their way to the global market place looking for cyber-gold. Does history repeat itself or what?

Even though the internet hasn't been the cash cow I hoped it would be. It is however, an excellent tool as an online portfolio. Once you set up your internet site with your art, it's there to be viewed 24/7. When you have new works of art, just add them to the site.

When people hear about you and want to see your art, or you want someone to look at your body of work, instead of mailing a printed brochure or tear sheet to them, have them look at your internet site. Then if they want to see a better reproduction of some of your work you can send them prints, tear sheets, or slides if you have them.

I advertise my website on the back of my prints and on my business cards. Most people have the internet and will use it to look you up. Most of my internet sales are from people who have already bought my art somewhere and want more, or they've seen me working on the street painting, received my business card and ordered later after they returned home.

Keep the internet in perspective, and realize you most likely won't get rich on it. In my experience, it's more valuable as a promotional tool.

If you decide to sell original art or reproductions of your art on your website, I recommend instead of purchasing an ecommerce package for accepting credit cards that you try using PayPal.

PayPal can be found at www.PayPal.com and it is the same system they use on Ebay.com for handling purchases. The advantage here is that if you don't have any sales, it doesn't cost you anything. They only charge a small fee when you have sales, otherwise it's free to set up and use.

I've had a website set up with a full ecommerce package before and it costs me $90.00 per month to have it. I paid that for a year because I was locked into a contract and only sold one print all year long for $125.00 - you do the math.

Building a Website

If you already have a website you are ahead of most artists. If you don't, let me share with you some options available for you to get one up and running.

Option #1

Have Someone who builds websites build one for you. If you don't want to take the time to learn how to build your own web page or don't know how to use a computer I recommend this option. You can find people who will build your website for as little as $399.00.

Option #2

Build your own website using word processor programs or graphic programs that have the ability to convert text and graphics into HTML web pages. Then upload the pages to a server (also called a host).

Sites that host other peoples web pages are ones like:

www.Hypermart.net
www.FreeServers.com
www.ThePrimeHost.com

There are even some programs available on the internet that will help you build web pages and some that will help you optimize your images so they load fast.

Option #3

Learn HTML code and buy software programs designed to make and maintain web pages and build a web site from the ground up. There are lots of software programs available to do this and lots of books written on how to build web pages, so I am not going to go into any detail here.

Search Engines

Here is the part of building a web page that most people miss. Once you have a web page built, you are online, but you are not in the global market place yet. Sure, if you tell someone you web address (http://members.aol.com/artist name.html) or (www.yourname.com), they can find your web site. Most people will never find you or know you exist on the web unless you are registered with a search engine.

Search engines are how people find what they are looking for on the internet. When someone sees your work, then later they go home and decide; "I really do like that painting - I'll look up the artist on the web." They go to a search engine, put in your name or the town they saw you in and the results are zero - zip - nothing. It's because search engines only search sites that are registered to be searched. I see this with artists web sites all the time.

Get Registered!

Getting registered is simple. You can do it yourself for free by going to a free submission site like: www.addme.com. There are lots of other places on the net that will submit your web site for you for a one time fee. Once you submit your web site the search engine will review your web site and see if it meets the criteria required to be listed.

The Criteria

You can skip to the next chapter if you are not building your own web site, but, make sure your web site builder includes title and meta tags in your web pages.

Here's what your web pages need to be accepted by the search engines = Title and Meta Tags!
Here is a sample, make sure these meta tags and code are above your HTML <BODY> code, and after the <HTML> code at the top of the page.

```
<HTML>
<HEAD>
<TITLE>Name, type of art etc.</TITLE>

<META                    NAME="description"
```

CONTENT= "Name - Type of Art - Location you live at etc. ">

<META NAME="keywords" CONTENT=" Name , kind of art , type of media , city , state, etc.">

</HEAD>
<BODY>

</BODY>
</HTML>

<Title>. - change text to "your name.-your type of art and town, state." (no more than 8 words)

<Meta-description> - Describe your site.
<Meta-keywords> - use your name, medium used, style of art, etc.....

From start to finish your HTML code should have these basic elements. Then there is no reason you should be refused by any search engine.

<HTML>
<HEAD>
<TITLE>Hawaii Artist Marshall White oil paintings & prints.</TITLE>

<META   NAME="description" CONTENT="Art paintings & prints by Hawaii artist Marshall White, online gallery

of Brian Marshall White. Kona, Hawaii.">

**<META   NAME="keywords"
CONTENT="**Big Island Artist , Art
Prints , Kona Artists , Hawaii Artists ,
Hawaii art , oil paintings , hawaiian art ,
big island artists , kona art , marshall
white , Brian Marshall White , Brian
White , underwater art , portraits , lan-
scapes , ">

</HEAD>
<BODY>

</BODY>
</HTML>

Now that you can be found on the search engines
when a customer types in your name or location,
you may want to fine tune your web page so people will find your web page just by typing in a
"keyword."

For example: "Atlanta Portrait Painter." If you're
a portrait painter in Atlanta, you want your web
site to be one that comes up on the first page of
the search engines results when some one types in
the keyword "Atlanta Portrait Painter."

Fine tuning your web page to do this takes lots of
time and some knowledge about how search engines operate. It can be done. The competition to

73

be on the first page of the results is often intense. Once you get "on top" it takes continual effort and adjusting your web page to stay "on top."

Another way to be on the first page is to join a directory that is already "on top" and let them do all the work to stay "on top" of the search engine results. For a small fee to be listed on the artists directory you get lots of exposure on the web without having to concentrate your efforts on your web pages search engine results.

To find a directory to join, type in a keyword in a search engine that people would use to find your kind of art.

For example: "Landscape artists," "Portrait Painters," "Seascape Painters," "Aviation Artists," and so on. On the first few pages of the search results see which ones are "artist directories." You want to be on the one that is closest to being #1. Compare membership fees if there is more than one directory. Some are much more expensive than others to join.

Chapter Ten
Small Print Reproductions

I will in this chapter, be sharing with you what equipment I use to make small print reproductions as well as the process of putting them together. I define "small prints" as 11x14 inch and smaller. The sizes I use are standard photography sizes of prints, matt boards and frames.

The Equipment

On the recommendation of other artists, I bought the Epson 2200 Stylus Photo Printer. It's not your standard desktop computer printer. It boasts the use of archival inks and produces professional quality prints. Most large computer supply stores sell the Epson 2200 Photo Stylus, if it is not on the shelf, you can order it.

Because it is a professional printer and not a standard desktop printer the inks are not carried by chain stores like Wal-Mart, K-Mart, or Costco. You will need to find out who the local supplier is for your local area or order online; www.SuppliesUSA.com is one online source. The printer can be purchased for anywhere between $650.00-$900.00. Keep in mind the price drops every year, so depending on how old this book is - it could be less.

For more information on the latest and the greatest printers out there for making prints of your art. Take a look at Wilhelm Imaging Research. Their web address is: www.Wilhelm-Research.com.

Other equipment you will need is: a computer and software programs. What kind of computer you get is up to you (Macintosh or P.C.). There are plenty of software graphic programs available for both. I have a P.C. (IBM based) computer and use Photoshop® and CorelDraw® software graphic programs to adjust and print my art prints.

Steps of Print Making Process

1. Digital image of artwork
2. Adjust in Photoshop®
3. CorelDraw® - Size and print
4. Mat boards & backing boards
5. Matting & signing prints
6. Artist bio sheet
7. Packaging prints

Digital Image of Artwork

To start out with, you should have a digital image of your art. No matter which process you use to get a digital image, you will want to compare printing it as it is, to how it prints out after you adjust the image in Photoshop. Most of the time I have found my art prints look better after being adjusted.

Sometimes multiple adjustments need to be made to achieve a satisfactory finished product and sometimes the original image will have to be re-scanned using a better process of getting a digital image of your original work of art. Also, keep in mind exact replication isn't always possible. Some digital cameras and printers aren't able to get certain colors, so get as close as possible.

Some companies who scan images of art also offer a calibration service. They usually for a fee will calibrate the scanned digital images to print on your type of printer. For the most part, this can save you lots of time making your own adjustments in Photoshop, but sometimes small adjustments still need to be made since calibrating is more of an art of estimating than it is an exact science.

Always have your images made into .TIF files and save them as .TIF files after adjusting them. If you can't get your artwork made into a digital .TIF file, have them made into a JPEG files (.JPG) . A .TIF file is the largest and clearest digital graphic file type available. It also is the only one that doesn't lose it's quality when saved time and time again.

A .JPG file is a lower quality, smaller file type than a .TIF and won't produce as good a print when making larger sized prints. It also loses its sharpness little by little each time it is adjusted and saved.

Never use a .BMP file, this file is too low of a quality file type to be used for making art prints.

Making Adjustments in Photoshop®

Open the digital image of your art in Photoshop® and rotate it if needed. Now, before you crop the image to the exact size of your art and get rid of the other stuff you don't want around the artwork itself, save it in a folder as "FileName_1" (or what ever name you choose).

Now, adjust the image by clicking on "Auto-Levels." Auto-Levels will measure all of the image file data and adjust the color and contrast automatically. Do this before you crop the image. Cropping the image first changes the overall file data and therefore changes the results you get from "Auto Levels." I struggled with wrong colors and too much purple in my prints before I discovered this trick.

Now, crop the image if needed and save the file as "FileName_2."

NOTE: If Photoshop® won't let you save the file you are working on as a .TIF file type, and it will only let you save it as .PSD (Photoshop file), you must click on "Flatten Image" and then save the file as a .TIF.

If you are using the Epson Stylus Photo 2200 and have loaded the software for the printer, you may have noticed other options for download on the disk that came with the printer. One of those options is "Install ICC Profiles." Choose this option and install it on your PC or Mac. When you are using PhotoShop and have opened an image to adjust, you can use the ICC profiles to automatically adjust your image for printing on the Epson 2200. It works great and has saved me lots of time!

To use the ICC profiles in Photoshop®; select image/mode/profile to profile. Then select your Epson printer and PhotoShop does the adjustment. Nine times out of ten, that's all I have to do to get a good print of my art.

There are many other ways to make adjustments in Photoshop and there are many ways to adjust colors individually, it's up to you to learn as much as you can about this massive graphic tool and use that knowledge to your benefit.

At this point you are done working in Photoshop unless you choose to print directly from Photoshop.

I haven't used Photoshop® Elements, but have heard from others that for the kind of use I've described here, it works just as well and cost less.

Using CorelDraw®

Several people have asked me why I don't just print right out of Photoshop®. Here is my answer; I personally found CorelDraw® easier to use when it comes to sizing my art and printing. It's not uncommon for professional printers to use different programs for printing and because I had used CorelDraw® before I started printing my art, it was an easy transition. With CorelDraw® I can see the size of the paper on the screen, make guidelines to size my image to, and print. What I see on the screen is what I get on the paper as far as print size goes, and that's important when you are trying to make every image the right size to fit the hole size in your mat boards. I also use Corel-Draw® to design and print my bio sheets, business cards and all of my promotional materials.

To start out you need to make three templates for your three print sizes: 5x7, 8x10 & 11x14. When you open CorelDraw® to the new page, the paper size you see there should be a 8.5x11 inch in size. To the top and left, there should be a ruler for measuring, if not, turn on "rulers" under the "view" options tab. Click on the ruler to the left and drag it over to the paper, do it again and then twice from the top ruler. Form a box area 8 inch by 10 inch. Save as "8x10_Template."

JEAN, AERI P

Unclaim : 10/6/2014

Held date   : 9/28/2014
Pickup location : Tigard Public Library

Title   : Breaking into the art world :
how to start making a living as an artist
Call number   : 702.3 WHI
Item barcode   : 33614033867374
Assigned branch : Beaverton City Library

Notes:

Here is a sample of how mine looks:

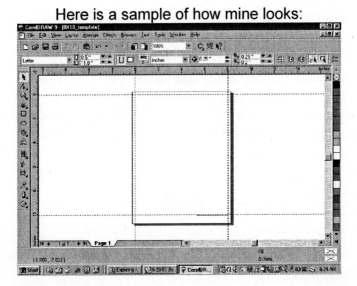

Do the same again, this time making two boxes on one page, each being 5x7 inch in size. Save it as "5x7_Template."

Sample:

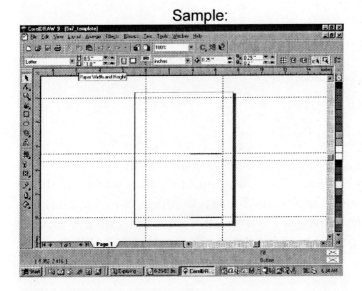

Now, click on "File" / "New" and make the last template. This time change the paper size from 8.5x11 to 11.7x16.5 (which happens to be the paper size of the large A3 paper you will need to print on to get your 11x14 prints). Now, make the rulers forming a box like you did before, this time make the box 11x14 inch in size. Save as "11x14_Template."

Sample:

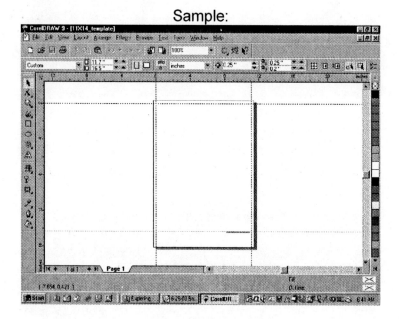

Now you have your base templates for sizing your images to print, always keep them and don't save over them, this way your prints always print the same size no matter what image you use. This is important to getting all your different art images to fit the mat boards you've ordered.

Before you start importing images to put in the templates, take a minute to open each template and type in small text your copyright information.....(c) Copyright (year) Artist Name, and save each template with the copyright info on it. This way you don't forget to add the copyright, it's always on the template from the start.

Adding Art Images to Templates

Open your 8x10_Template.cdr. Click on "File/ Import," choose the art image that looks best and import it. (If you haven't test printed your art images, do it now and choose the best one.) Once it's imported, click on the image and then click and drag the little square nodes on the corners to size it and then move it into place. Zoom in to get a closer look at the corners and line up the edge of your art image with the inside of the box you created on the template.

Depending on the size of your original image, you may need to re-crop it in Photoshop so it fits or simply stretch it to fit your box in CorelDraw. You can get away with some stretching, I do and most people never notice it, but when it comes to having round objects in your art (like a moon), stretching will show, so cropping is a better choice.

Now that it fits your 8x10 inch box size, save your new file as FileName_8x10. Do the same with the other templates, importing and saving them also.

You should now have three different files ready to open and print.

Printer Paper

Experimenting with different brands of printer photo paper is a good idea. Using the correct printer options (choosing the right option to match the type of paper) will make a big difference in how your prints come out. I suggest you make your own test results, and once you've decided to go with one kind of paper, stick to it. Changing paper can change the color of your prints and you will have to re-adjust your images to print out the right color again.

Having said that, here is what I use after doing some testing of my own. I use 8.5x11 Epson Glossy Photo Paper (52 lb.), it's a heavy paper which helps resist any waviness you get with thinner photo papers caused by changes in humidity.

For my 11x14 prints I use 11.7x16.5 Epson Matte Paper - Heavyweight (#S041260).

Good luck and happy printing.

Chapter Eleven
Mat Boards and Matting

Many artists I know have made their own mat boards at one time or the other, I even have my own mat board cutter.

Let me ask you a question; How do you want to spend your time? Would you rather be doing your art or making mat boards? Making your own mats is expensive and time consuming, calculate the costs of buying sheets of mat board and the time it takes to cut it into mats, then compare it to buying pre-cut mats in bulk. I think you will see your time is better spent making art.

There are several sources around the country you can buy pre-cut mat boards from, most will make them any size you want. I buy my mats from Frames Central in Portland, Oregon. Their website is www.Documounts.com.

I suggest choosing one color mat board and sticking with it for all of your prints. Having a selection of different mats can be a headache and stocking multiple colors in bulk can be expensive.

One problem with having different mats is if the texture isn't the same and someone wants to buy two or more prints, they complain about the fact that the texture on one mat is different than the other, and ask if you can switch mats with something else.

Another problem, if you have more than one color of mat available, some of your buyers will say, "Oh, I like this picture, can I see how it looks in this other color mat?" Now you're swapping mat boards and wasting time better spent selling to others or making your art. This can be a real pain if you're selling on the street or working a booth. I suggest, have only one color and tell them they can easily change the mat color at their local frame shop.

I don't sell my art prints with frames for the same reason, people can be picky and hard to please when it comes to choosing a frame to match their house. Once you start, you're suddenly in the framing business trying to stock different kinds of frames to please different people. I'm not in the framing business, to do so would take my focus off of my art.

Mat Board Sizes and Hole Sizes

Choose your mat hole sizes carefully, once you set up all your art print files to print a certain size, it's a lot of work to go back later and change your art print sizes to match a new hole size. Imagine realizing you could have made a better choice on hole size so you didn't have to stretch your art prints as much or at all, but to make the change now, you'd have to change 150 files + and re-save them all. If starting over, I would choose a more symmetrical looking mat, even all the way around.

Here are the mat boards I buy (not that you should order the same hole size):

The kind of mat I buy is a "Canterbury," the color is Bright White.

8x10 frame size mat has a hole size of 4.75 x 6.75 inches. For a backing board I buy a 8x10 product called X-Board, which is about the same thickness as the mat board itself.

11x14 frame size mat has a hole size of 7.5 x 9.5 inches. For a backing board I buy 11x14 x 1/8 inch foam core board. It's just thick enough to be sturdy for display purposes, but not too thick to go into a frame.

16x20 frame size mat has a hole size of 10.75 x 13.75 inches. For a backing board I buy 16x20 x 1/8 inch foam core board.

If you can't figure out what hole size you want or need, you can always ask what the standard hole size is used by others who order mats.

Matting your Prints

When I first started, I would use spray glue to mount my prints to my backboards. Not only is this toxic and messy - it's time consuming! Besides, the glues would often fail and the prints would get wavy with temperature changes.

The best way which happens to be the fastest way is the "Hinged Method." The hinged method is the most widely used method for mounting prints to back boards. For this you will need artists tape, which you can buy at your local art store, if not, you can buy it at Frames Central.

Step 1;
Working on a flat surface like a desk or table, Lay your mat backboard down and your print on top. Then take your mat board and lay it on top. Make sure the sides and the corners of the mat and the backboard line up all the way around.

Step 2;
Your goal here is to hold the mat board in place, moving only the print inside into position. You want the print centered with the covered area on the sides of the print equal all the way around. This way if your mat moves while in the package, there won't be any white paper showing.

Step 3;
Now, holding one side down, gently use your other hand to push the print into place. When you have

the print centered so that no white is showing, carefully hold the print in place and move the mat down exposing the top of the print.

Step 4;
Take your artists tape and tear a piece the same width as the top of the print and tape the top of the print down to the backboard. Don't tape the sides or the bottom, your print needs to be free to expand with temperature and humidity.

Place your mat back on top and even up the edges, make sure the print is still in position. If not, remove the tape and try again.

Here are some photos of the process:

Step 1: Even outer edges of mat with backing.

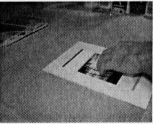

Step 2 & 3: Position, hold and slide mat down.

Step 4: Tear tape and tape top down to back.

Notice I'm using my pinkies to hold mat down, this helps to keep the print from moving while I tape it into position.

Chapter Twelve
Signing Your Art and Prints

When I first started, my question was, "Where's the right place to sign my art?" I've seen signatures all over, but most sign their art on the bottom right hand corner of the print. I've seen some who don't sign the print itself, but sign the mat board just below the right hand corner (mostly photographers). I don't recommend doing this. If you do and they decide to change mats to another color, your signature is gone with the old mat board.

For the purpose of promoting your art, sign it with your name and make it readable. When people see a piece of art on the wall and they like it, they usually look to see who the artist is. Your art is now advertising your name to art lovers and the more people who see your name, the more familiar you become to the art buying public.

In my opinion, artists who sign their art with a symbol, initials or a scribble you can't read are only hurting themselves.

When signing originals, sign them with a copy-right symbol, year and name.
Example: ©2005 Artist Name
When you make prints, just sign your name.

One thing to consider when reproducing your art is your signature. Instead of having your signature on the print twice (one from the original signature on the painting and one you hand sign on the print), digitally remove your original signature in PhotoShop before you make the print. Better yet, have the scan of your painting done before you sign the original, then make prints. You can sign the original work of art later.

I've done it both ways and having one signature on the print looks much better. I've actually had people not buy my art because it had the original signature and the hand signed signature on the print over it. People want to know the print is hand signed by the artist, so be sure to hand sign your prints.

If you are selling to art prints to tourists, you may want to also make a reference to where you are or where the scene is. For example, I'm in Hawaii, so I write "Hawaii" on the bottom left hand corner of the print.

Some artists have told me "that's stupid" and I shouldn't do it because people buying the art know where it is. But, my experience is most people want their print to say where it is. When I didn't have the state on it, I was getting requests all the time for me to write Hawaii on them anyway.

Tourists mostly buy smaller 5x7 or 8x10 prints, so I always put Hawaii on these sizes, tourists like it and it saves me the time it takes to do it on location. I've never had a customer yet say "I want this print, but do you have one without the name Hawaii on it?" For my larger prints, I never put the name Hawaii on them anymore, if they request it, then I do it for them.

Limited Edition Prints

Having limited editions of your prints is a good idea. I didn't have any at first and soon found out that some people won't buy unless the prints are limited editions.

Having limited editions is a lot of extra work for the artist. You have to keep a record of how many prints you've sold and you have to provide a certificate of authenticity stating how many prints the edition is limited to, and what number in the edition this particular print is. Once you have sold all the limited edition prints in that size, you can't and shouldn't make any more.

Here is what I've done considering my own situation. Since I sell to tourists and I paint locations that are familiar, some of my images I can still be selling ten years from now, so I don't want to make them limited editions. Both my smallest sizes are open edition prints, my largest size art paper prints and my Giclée canvas prints are all limited editions. My feeling is, if they are collectors and want limited editions, they will have to buy my $65.00 prints or my higher priced Giclée canvas prints.

Some Giclée makers provide certificates and will help you keep track of how many you have made. For your small art paper prints, you will have to make your own. There are certificate papers you can buy at office supply stores and then you can just print the text you want on them. I make my own in CorelDraw®.

Here is a sample of mine, it's more than you need, but I wanted mine to be unique:

It has the size of print, title of print, a place to fill in the edition number, number in the edition, date original painting was made and a place to sign the certificate. Two of these fit on a 8 1/2x11 sheet of paper. The date of purchase and place of purchase I just leave blank and let the customer fill that in later.

After printing them out, I number and sign each one and file them with my bio sheets for that particular print title. As I print my art prints out later, I then pull them from the file and attach them to the back of the art print. (For info on attaching certificates to back of prints, see chapter 13).

When you sign your name on your limited edition prints, also write the number and number of the edition.
Example:
Artist Signature 2/200

The number you sign on the print should always match the number on the certificate.

What to sign prints with

I use a gold paint pen made by "Pilot." Pilot gold marker - extra fine point. You can usually find them in office supply stores. The gold is classic and most artists I know use gold paint pens to sign their prints. Hint: Always shake well and test write on scrap paper before signing your print.

I've ruined more than a few prints by not test writing first. Sometimes a glob of paint will flood out of the pen, so test write first each time before signing.

Chapter Thirteen
Artist Bio Sheet

People have a desire for information, and here is where you not only fulfill their desire for information, but you promote yourself as an artist and promote your work. This is something few artists pay attention to, either because they don't care or they don't know how important it is.

If you just type your artists info out on a typewriter, copy it and slap it on the back of your print, you've done the minimum possible.

Presentation matters!

Making an eye catching bio sheet is easy. A good presentation on the back of your art print makes a big impression on people and can give you the edge you need to sell more than the other guy.

The size of this bio sheet is 5 inch by 7 ½ inch, it's small enough to print two on a page of regular paper and it fits on the back of my small 8x10 mat boards.

Here is a sample of mine, I used CorelDraw® to make this one:

St. Peters Sunset

St. Peters Church also called "The Little Blue Church".
Located in Kona on Ali'i Drive on the north side of Kahalu'u Beach Park - Big Island, Hawaii. This church is the most photographed church on the island.

This Print is a reproduction of an original oil painting done in January 2002.

Brian Marshall White

Discover for yourself the beauty and depth of this Big Island artist. Each painting takes you on a journey to experience the wonders of Hawaii.

About the Artist

A Florida native, Marshall White is a self-taught artist who finds his inspiration from the natural landscape. During his 18-year career as a sign painter, he painted with oils mainly as a hobby; portraits of people, landscapes and seascapes. Marshall had his first exhibition since high school at the age of 39 in the Port of Seattle's First annual Art Show (2000).

In May of 2001 Marshall re-located to Kona, Hawaii with his wife and children to pursue his art full time. He produces beautiful paintings from his studio in his home and at his street location on Ali'i drive in Kailua Kona.
The subject of his paintings include scenes of Hawaii, wildlife and portraits of people.

Marshall's original oils and prints are on display in various stores and galleries on Hawaii and Maui.

Marshall White Fine Art
PO Box 1555
Kailua-Kona, HI 96745

Phone: (XXX) XXX-XXXX
SuccessfulArtist@aol.com

www.BrianMarshallWhite.com

MARSHALL WHITE

There are several basic things you want on your bio sheet.

1. A short biography
2. A photo of the artist
3. The title of the art print
4. A short description of what the art is about and/or it's location
5. Print Statement
6. Contact information
7. Web address
8. Promotional blurb

A Short Biography

Take a look around at how other artists have written their biographies. Things to include are:

- Where you are from
- What you use to do
- Your art education
- What medium you work in
- Where you live and work now
- Where your art can be viewed

Always write as if someone else wrote it about you.

Photo of the Artist

Be sure to put a photo of yourself on your bio sheet, photos put a face with the name. People want to see who the artist is, it answers the question, "What does the artist look like?" and makes your art more appealing because now that they have seen you, you seem more personable.

The Title of the Art Print

Put the title of the art at the top of the bio sheet in bold letters. This is the first thing they will want to know when looking at the print.

A Short Description

Below the title, write what the art is about or if it is a location, write about the location. Provide any historical information if it has historical significance. Also where the location is (city, state, etc.).

Print Statement

This is important. Some people can't tell if what they are looking at is a art print, original painting or a photograph and they will feel deceived if they buy it thinking it's an original painting and find out later it is only a print reproduction.

If you don't do painting, write what medium you use to make the original work of art.

Here is what I do, I add the date the original was made. Example: "This Print is a reproduction of an original oil painting created in July of 2003."

I do this because sometimes I get asked, "When did you do the original?" Having the answer on the back of the print provides information to buyer and to me, because I often can't remember exactly when I painted something.

Contact Information

Provide your business name and/or your name, address and (optional) phone number. Also provide your email address if you have one.

Web Address

Having a web address lets people know your art is on display on the internet, this can lead to additional sales later.

Promotional Blurb

It's often hard to write your own promotional blurb, getting help from another person or several others will help. Ask this question; "How would you describe me and my work if your were to write about me for a newspaper article?"

The responses you get are usually insightful and encouraging. Use the feedback to put together your own promotional statement about the artist. A promotional blurb is like a testimony of how people see you and your style of art.

Here is what another artist wrote about me, I thought it was well done and it wasn't something I would have written myself.

"Big Island Artist Marshall White paints wonderfully detailed and realistic oil paintings of familiar Hawaiian locations. His works are so engaging that you feel you could step right into the scene."

Some artists make one bio sheet for all prints because it's much easier. You can do this, but you won't be able to put the title and info about each individual work of art on it. I worked in a co-op gallery for awhile where other artists have generic bio sheets, people ask all the time about their work, "Where is this?" and "What's the title?" I didn't do the art, and I don't know. The print itself has no information to promote itself, so I can't answer them.

A good bio sheet will provide all the basic information needed to answer common questions asked about the artist and the art.

Attaching the Bio Sheet

Trim the bio sheet to size, I use a regular paper cutter. Then glue it on the back of the backing board. I've tried spray glue, glue sticks and finally decided regular Elmer's Glue-All® works best. If your print is a limited edition art paper print, glue the certificate of authenticity just below the bio sheet also.

Chapter Fourteen
Packaging your prints

To protect your prints and the mat boards from getting damaged, you need to seal them up in plastic. There are two ways of doing this,

1. Shrink wrap them
2. Buy plastic sleeves or bags that seal

I've done both and can tell you from experience that using plastic clear bags is not only easier, but your prints look better, making a better presentation.

When I first started I invested $500.00 to buy a shrink wrap machine and material needed. Using the shrink wrap system takes a lot of time and it's hard to get a good seal. Often, the sealed edges would fail when heated to shrink or would fail later when people handled them to look at them. About one out of every 5 would fail, that's when I decided to switch over to using clear bags for my prints. Also, the electricity used to heat the machine and heat gun is an additional cost.

Plastic sleeves (aka clear bags) is the best way to package your art prints. They're not expensive, you don't need any special equipment to seal them and they can be re-opened and re-sealed without destroying the clear plastic sleeve.

People often want the artist to personalize the print by writing a short note, signing and dating it on the back. With the clear bags you can do this, with the shrink wrap, you can't.

You can buy clear bags in almost any size you need. I get mine from Impact Images www.Clearbags.com, you can call them (1-800-223-2630) and order by phone also. If you are ordering from Frames Central (www.Documounts.com), you can buy them there also.

Ask about sizes and explain how thick your prints are to get the right sizes. They usually sell them in packs of 100.

I use for 8x10 mats:
#B108PC, Size= 8 7/16 x 10 1/4

For 11x14 mats:
#B11PC, Size= 11 7/16 x 14 1/4

For 16x20 mats:
#B16PC, Size= 16 7/16 x 20 1/8

The ones I order have the sticky part on the bag itself, rather than on the flap. I do this because if you have the sticky part on the flap, when you or the customer removes the print, sometimes the flap sticks to the print which pulls the ink off and ruins the print. I've done it myself and had customers call me and complain that they ruined their print. Of course, to make them happy, I send them another. This adds up as lost revenues fast if it happens too much.

Presentation

I've said it before and I'll say it again, presentation matters!

By having a nice presentation you add value to your art. Think of it this way; You do a drawing or a watercolor on a 8x10 piece of paper, if you stick it on a your refrigerator , it has one presentation value. If you mount it and mat it and put it in a frame on the wall, it has another presentation value. Which way of presenting the art to the viewer says the art is worth more?

I've seen artists mount prints to colored card stock with no mat board, and then wrap it with cellophane food wrap you use in your kitchen!

If you value your art enough to present it well, customers will also value your art.

Another part of presentation is display. Your prints should be setup in such a way that they are easy to reach, see and thumb through. If your customer has to reach or kneel on the ground to look at your art, you make physically hard for them to relax and enjoy your art. This will cause them to move on to viewing something else that isn't so physically straining to view.

For displays to hold your art prints, use clear Plexiglas bins. That way people can see through the Plexiglas and portions of your art isn't covered completely. Prints sit nicely and it makes it easy for people to flip through. Avoid using cardboard boxes or laying a stack of prints flat on the table top. Doing the later requires them to use both hands to thumb through your art, many shoppers already have one hand full and aren't always willing to set their stuff down.

Most large cities have shops that manufacture Plexiglas bins, if not you can order them online.

For the larger 16x20 mat size prints you can use a fold up display bin. Most art stores carry them or can order them for you.

Some consignments shops and galleries are more organized than others, many have their own display equipment. For the ones that don't, providing your own insures your art will have a nice presentation.

Chapter Fifteen
Giclée Reproductions

Once you've started making money on your small prints, consider investing some of that money back into the business by having Giclée prints made of your art.

If you've been selling your small prints for a few months, you should already have a good idea by now which images are your most popular and which ones aren't. Obviously, you'll want to make Giclée prints of your best sellers first.

The most common Giclée prints are art paper & canvas. Giclée makers have options when it comes to materials to print on, so you should talk with them about which materials are best for you.

There are different canvas textures. Some Giclée makers clear coat and some don't. If you intend to enhance your print by painting on the print, you should make sure the canvas and clear coat they use will allow you to paint over it.

When choosing a company to scan and make Giclées of your art, be sure they will give you a copy of the original scan on a disk. Some companies won't. You need a copy of the original scan to make your small prints on your own printer. If they refuse to give you a copy of the scan each time you have your art scanned, don't use them, find someone else to do your scans and Giclées.

Ask other artists in your area who they use, because not all printers are equal in quality, I have used several local Giclée printmakers and can tell you from experience that some have better scanning technology than others and some have better printing technology than others.

Giclée Printmakers

I use Kona Giclée here in Hawaii, but you can find other Giclée printmakers by simply doing a search on the internet. Here are a few Giclée printmakers in the United States that you might consider using if you can't find one locally:

California:
Duganne Ateliers, (310)314-0050
2651 Main Street
Santa Monica, CA 90405
http://www.duganne.com
Jack Duganne

Jack works with a large variety of local artists, some self published, others just experimenting, and others who are represented. He actually invented the term Giclée in the early '90s after many years as a professional fine art serigrapher.

Eclipse Workshop Collectors Editions, (818)885-0788
9002 Eton Avenue
Canoga Park, CA 91304-1616
http://www.collectorseditions.com
Tim Dixon
They publish and print many well known artists.

Nash Editions, (310)545-4352
2317 N. Sepulveda Blvd.
Manhattan Beach, CA 90266
http://www.nasheditions.com
Mac Holbert
They specialize in photography and were the first in the industry. David Coons of ArtScans was actually an original co-founder of Nash Editions in 1990. They handle a large number of big name photographers, and are particularly good at black and white.

Opus Editions, (818)779-0933
5934 Kester
Van Nuys, CA 91411
http://www.opuseditions.com
Maroun Sahyoun
Maroun has been doing fine art reproduction for many years. His clients are extremely satisfied with his work.

Art Works, (626)449-3840
130 N. Marengo Ave.
Pasadena Ca 91101
http://fineartpublishing.com
Scott Williamson
Scott was an expert color corrector for Harvest Productions for many years before he started his own fine art printing company, which subsequently merged with Art Works in Pasadena.

Pangea Editions, (949)916-5784
24335 Regina St.
Mission Viejo, CA 92691
http://www.pangeaeditions.net
Curtis Wibe
Curtis runs his own business after working with Irvine Lithographics and Harvest Products. He has an excellent mastery of color management and an attention to detail.

Hawaii:
Maui Giclée, (800)-818-6189
http://www.mauigiclee.com

Studio Gi'Clique, Inc., (808) 261-0100
1619 Ulueo
Kailua, HI 96734

Massachusetts:
Singer Editions, (617) 423-3484
300 Summer Street #44
Boston, MA 02210
http://www.singereditions.com

Rhode Island:
Blazing Editions, (401)885-4329
PO box 1954
East Greenwich, RI 02818
http://www.blazing.com
Alan Blazar
He's been publishing a select collection of artists around the country and has both Iris and I-Jet printers. He has color management fairly well under control and has managed to assemble a fairly high volume studio.

Washington State:
Aris Editions, 1-877-340-2747
www.ariseditions.com,

Art Scanning Services:
ArtScans Studio, (310)-313-3000
www.artscans.com,
David Coons /owner.
Caroline Dockrell /Production Manager
11924 W. Jefferson Blvd, Ste A
Culver City, CA 90230

ArtScans doesn't make Giclées, but they are famous for their ability to get the highest quality scan possible. Many hire ArtScans to do their scanning and then hire another company to do their Giclée printing.

Another option to using a company who makes Giclée prints is to buy your own Giclée printer.

You can hire a company like ArtScans to scan your original work of art and then have them profile it for your printer. You can make your own Giclée reproductions on paper or canvas. There are lots of Giclée printers out there to consider, but take a look at the Roland and the Epson Giclée printers. My Giclée printmaker uses the Roland and a artist friend of mine owns the Epson 9600 and does some really impressive Giclées with it.

There is a learning curve to printing your own Giclées, and you will have to decide for your own situation if the investment of time and money is worth it.

For more information on the Giclée printing process and instruction in the latest digital printing techniques, take a look at Harald Johnson's book titled *"Mastering Digital Printing, Second Edition."* ISBN: 1-59200-431-8 © 2005 Publish date: October 26, 2004. His web site is: www.dpandi.com.

Choosing Paper or Canvas

One school of thought is that if you paint in oils, acrylics, or another similar medium that you can make reproductions on canvas, paper or both. If you paint in watercolors, pastels, draw or another similar medium that you should only make Giclée reproductions on paper.

But, with recent sales that I've heard about, the canvas print has become the most popular choice among art buyers. Many artists are even discontinuing to make art paper Giclée prints because they have so many more sales with the canvas prints.

With this new trend, a new school of thought is starting to gain momentum that says; It doesn't matter what medium you use, if canvas prints sell better, make canvas prints of your art. Time will tell how far and wide this will go and if the art buying public will go along.

I have chosen to just make canvas prints for now, leaving myself the option to make lithograph or paper Giclée prints of my images later on when I gain popularity.

Giclée makers usually charge by the square inch after the initial setup and scan. The cost is usually between 10 cents to 20 cents per square inch for canvas prints.

To Enhance or Not to Enhance

If you choose to have canvas Giclée prints made of your art images, the next question is whether or not to enhance them. Enhancing a canvas is simply hand highlighting areas with the medium like oils or acrylics. I use oils for the original painting, so I enhance with oils.

Some artists don't enhance their prints, some do. My experience is; if you enhance a print, you can charge more for it and when selling, being able to say, "This Giclée has been hand highlighted by the artist" adds value to the piece and sometimes makes the sale.

When enhancing, the rule of thumb is to not spend more than fifteen minutes doing it. But, I've spent hours getting a print the way I want it.

More on Limited Editions / Open Editions

Most people who buy Giclée prints want them to have collection value. Meaning, when you get famous, their print of your art will be worth more.

I recommend making all of your Giclées limited editions and only having open editions on your posters and small art paper prints. That way you can make all the small prints you want without having to keep track of them. People who only spend 20 or 30 bucks usually aren't buying art for collection value, those who invest several hundred dollars usually are.

How limited should your limited editions be? That really is up to you, but I've discovered by talking with collectors that they prefer to buy small editions (100 in the edition or less). I started out making my canvas Giclée editions 450, but now I never make them higher than 100 in the edition.

I now make two sizes of limited editions from some of my larger paintings. If the full size is 22x30, I make only 50 limited editions of it. Then I make a smaller size 16x22 and only make 100 limited editions of it.

Preparing to be Collected

Collectors are looking for several things when buying Giclées.

1. Signed and numbered
2. Documentation
3. If enhanced - notation of enhancement

Sign your print with a gold pen and number it. (See Chapter 12 on signing prints).

The documentation they are looking for is a "certificate of authenticity." This can be a full size sheet of paper or a half size sheet. The certificate should state the following information;

- Certificate of Authenticity
- Print size
- Title
- Artist name
- Edition number
- Year painted
- Statement: I hereby certify the accompanying piece of art is represented as stated above
- Signature
- Artist address, website, etc.

Here is a sample of one I use for Giclée prints. It's similar to the ones I use for my large art paper prints, but it's full color and printed on good quality paper or glossy card stock.

If you enhance your Giclées, you should ink stamp on the back of the print a statement saying something to the effect:

"This canvas Giclée print hand-highlighted and enhanced by: Artist name."
Then sign it with your signature and date it.

I bought a self re-inking stamp for this. I custom ordered it with the text I wanted. You should be able to find a local company to do this for you also, or try www.Staples.com.

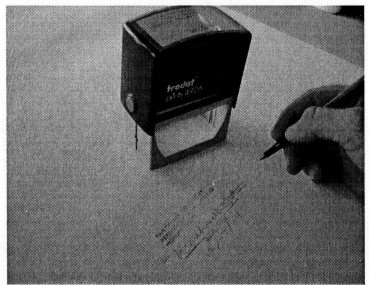

Ink stamp and signature on back of Giclées.

Note on Clear Coats

Before you enhance your Giclée print with oils or acrylic, you should clear coat the print. Talk to your Giclée maker about what kind of clear coat is best for the process they use to print.

If your Giclée maker does the clear coat for you, then you don't have to worry about this process.

Note on Shipping

Shipping Giclée prints are easier if you sell them before they are stretched over stretcher bars. This isn't always possible, but when you can you'll find the shipping is a lot cheaper. Most of the galleries I work with prefer me to ship them the Giclée prints un-stretched. They then take it to a framer and have it stretched and framed.

For shipping originals or stretched Giclée prints (framed or unframed), take a look at cardboard crates made by Airfloat Systems Inc. called "Strong Boxes." They are lightweight and re-usable. Their web site is www.airfloatsys.com. Phone: 1.800.445.2580.

Chapter Sixteen
Pricing Originals

Pricing originals isn't easy, you have to start out and see what the market will bear. Some try to price them too high and their work just sits around and never sells. On the other hand if you are pricing them too low, you will know it because they will be selling as fast as you can make them. That is how you find what the market will bear.

If they are selling really well, it's time to mark them up a little, when you mark them up to a place where they aren't moving, then you've gone too high. Try to find a good middle ground where you are making a good profit and they are still moving.

I have paintings I've done that to me are worth more than I can get for them, those paintings I hold onto until the value of my work goes up. I can sell them later and get my asking price. In my first year of selling full time, I had a painting that was 24x30 inches, I was only asking $500. for it and it was a nice piece titled "Bird of Paradise." A guy wanted to buy it but only wanted to pay $200.

for it, I wouldn't sell it for that so he left. Two years later, I still have it and am selling paintings that size for $1,800. On a regular basis and could easily sell it now for more than twice my original asking price. My wife likes it so much, she doesn't want me to sell it, so for her it hangs in our bedroom.

To make pricing simple and for the purpose of having a standard, there is a easy way to price all of your originals. Once you have found what the market will bear and you know what a 16x20 normally sells for, figure how many square inches a 16x20 painting is. Calculate the asking price divided by the square inches and you will get a per inch price for selling your originals.

Example: Let's say you usually sell a 16x20 inch painting for $500.00. A 16x20 painting is 320 square inches.

$500. Divided by 320 = $1.56 per square inch.

Now you have a standard per inch price to charge for your originals, so if you want to price a 24x30 inch painting all you have to do is times the square inches by $1.56 per square inch.

24x30= 720 square inches
720 x $1.56 = $1,123.20

This is a good thing to do when working with galleries that sell your art, especially if they are trying to sell a commission for you to paint. If they know your per square inch selling price, they can calculate and quote the customer without ever having to call you and ask a price. They can close a sale faster, which is good for both you and the gallery. Remember, what ever percent you have negotiated with the gallery for is the same percent you get of your per square inch price.

That brings me to something else to consider when pricing your art. Your retail per square inch price should be the same as they would sell it for in a gallery. If you aren't working with a gallery then it's no big deal. But when you do start working with a gallery, your retail prices and their retail prices should be the same no matter who is buying.

To have a gallery that is selling your work is great, and if they are selling and making you money, you don't want to undercut them by selling stuff out of your studio for half the price. The galleries get a little touchy about that kind of thing and besides, if they drop your art because of it, you'd be cutting your own throat.

You have your reputation in the art community to think about. One gallery selling your art can lead to another and another and another, pretty soon you will have a good income coming in and lots of steady work. On the other hand if you get a reputation for undercutting the galleries you work with, word will spread and what would have been great opportunities will be opportunities missed.

I have a price for original oils and a different price for original acrylics. I consider my oils to be my more serious work and my acrylic paintings more of a money maker with tourists.

Chapter Seventeen
Where to Start

"Hind sight is twenty/twenty." Having experienced many mistakes in my own approach to becoming a full-time artist, I would do things a little different if I had it to do over again. It is with that experience that I share with you my opinions on what to do first to reach your goal to becoming a full time artist.

This is not a prescription for success, nor is it an exact science. Success comes with lots of hard work, long hours and thoughtful investments of time, energy and money. There are many variables that effect the results you will get, and it's possible that you may have to try a different approach to achieve your own goal of becoming a full-time artist.

My opinions are only meant to be a general guideline to aid you in making your own decisions about how to invest your own time, energy and money. I can only hope the insights and experiences I've shared with you in this book will be helpful in some way.

That Annoying Thing Called Overhead

Any good business person will tell you it's not going to happen overnight, so don't quit your day job just yet. You are about to build a business of making and selling art, and businesses take time to establish. I recommend keeping your full-time job and doing your art on the side, as your art business grows and you start making sales that equal what you are taking home, then consider cutting back to part time.

As with any business, there are expenses, and you will be investing money to buy a printer, mat boards, bags, scans of your original works of art, and etc. Not to mention you have to maintain your current overhead
(food, shelter, vehicle and etc.).

First things First

One of the first things you'll want to do is study your art market in your area. Go into galleries and gift shops that sell art and find out what paintings and prints are the best sellers, and then find out why they sell so well.

The best way is to simply ask the sales person, they hear the comments made by customers and often have their own opinions about what sells best and why.

Be sure to talk to many different galleries and gift shops, some galleries have a reputation for selling "different' or "odd" art. Their opinions won't help you much if you are trying to find out what the tourists buy and what the majority of people buy in general.

If you are mostly selling small prints, you may get a better idea of what to paint talking to gift shops that sell small prints. I've actually had stores and galleries tell me what they are looking for and what they can sell best.

Once you get an idea of what kinds of paintings and prints sell well, it's time to build a body of work. Be careful not to duplicate anyone else's work, use your own style and your own creativity. The last thing you want is a lawsuit filed against you because you copied someone else's work from a greeting card or calendar.

That is why I do my own photography of locations I paint, it's mine from the start, and I don't have to worry about someone saying I copied their work. My feeling is; Life is too short, and I have too many of my own creative ideas that I want to do, I'm not going to waste my time copying someone else.

Second Things Second

Start making prints of your art. Depending on how much money you have to work with, you need to choose the process you are going to use to make prints of your work. If you start out making photo prints - that's fine, but work towards getting better equipment and better quality prints of your art eventually.

Buy your materials (mats, backing boards and clear bags to package them). Get what you need to put your prints together and have them ready to sell. The sooner you have prints to offer, the sooner you can start placing them in consignment shops and/or selling them on the street.

While in the process of getting the equipment and materials together, now is the time to do your research. If you are going to work on the street as a street artist, look for the "hot spots" to sell your art and locate the best consignment shops to approach with your product. If you are not going to work as a street artist, you can build a nice business on the side while working full time at your regular job. The shops are selling for you and if you get enough stores selling, it can be a good side income.

Third Things Third

Now that you are selling your art prints, continue to draw or paint new images to sell, build up your body of work and monthly add the new art prints to your sales and consignments.

Some will become your new best sellers and others will almost never sell. After a few months, if an image doesn't sell, discontinue to carry it. Pick out your best sellers and consider making Giclée reproductions of them. Adding Giclée canvas prints to your list of items for sale will increase your income as they begin to sell.

Try to build your art business, don't consume all the money it generates. Save money to buy materials and equipment needed. If you don't invest in your own art career - who will?

As you progress, get more consignments. Soon your art will be in all the best locations and when the busy tourist season hits, you will have a solid base for your business built to provide a good income.

During the busy season, set some money aside if you can and/or stock up on more supplies to get you through the slow season.

Join a co-op gallery or consign your originals at a local gallery. Find someplace nice to display and sell your originals.

Submit your art to greeting card companies, and other companies that will license your work.

Chapter Eighteen
Just a Few Comments

I've seen lots of artists come through where I live and some try to make money with their art. Many of those have quit before their art had a chance to sell. They quit all together instead of trying to figure out why their art isn't selling.

Art + location + price + season + economy = art sales.

It's an equation! If art sales are slow or you don't have any at all, figure out which part of the equation needs adjustment. Don't give up! Work on the equation. If you are going to sell your art, stick with it, be consistent. If selling your art is a passing thing, then why bother going to the expense?

Consistent people will triumph! Be consistent.

Sometimes the art we do, we like it and think, "This will sell well," but it doesn't. Paint or draw more and don't be discouraged, soon you will have one that sells great!

Sometimes it's not the art, sometimes it's a bad location, or it's a slow week, off season or and economic slump. Find out from other retailers if their sales are down. Sometimes my experience has been that jewelry is the hot seller of the week and art prints just aren't selling well at any one's stores. Other times, photographs are selling like crazy and then I have weeks where art prints are the hot sales item and I do really well.

The point is don't give up or be discouraged. Give locations a chance considering economic factors, try and try again. If you've given it a good go at one location without success, try another for awhile. Look at the equation and work on it.

The Artistic Personality

If you are a true artist at heart, you most likely have the same characteristics most artists have. I won't say you are a stereotypical artist type, because that's a negative view by people who don't understand the way artists think.

But, the truth is most artists including my self have an overflow of creativity coming out of them, and it comes out in many forms. We are multi-talented and can do many things well, and we want to experiment with our ideas. It's the bouncing from one idea to the other, from one project to the other, that gets us the stereotypical reputation.

We have to focus the creativity that flows through us. Staying focused takes discipline and a lot of effort, but unless we do, we find ourselves going in too many directions and then we don't succeed at anything. To succeed, you have to be consistent, choose a direction and stay focused on it.

I have had many creative ideas, some were good money making ideas and some were inventive ideas that would take lots of time and maybe never make me any money. I keep reminding myself to stay focused on the main thing I'm doing, so I can succeed at that. I allow myself a few side projects, but never let myself lose momentum on the main goal. I don't play guitar as much as I use too, this book is a side project, that is why it took me so long to finish it and get it published.

I understand it's hard for us artists, but if you want to succeed as a artist, you will have to constantly remind yourself of where you want to go with your art career and pick and choose carefully the side projects you take on. I always evaluate the projects I want to do and ask myself these questions; "Is this in the same direction as my main goal to be a full-time artist?" "Will it compliment what I am already doing or will it take my time away from my main goal?"

Galleries and people who collect art want to work with artists who are consistent, artists who will still be doing their art in five years. They want to know they can depend on you when they sell your work to provide more. They don't want to work with artists who are there one minute and gone on to something else the next.

It may take several years, but by sticking with your main focus and direction, you are proving to others that you are here to stay. You will get a reputation for being dependable rather than a reputation for being a flake.

The Bottom Line

There are too many variables involved for me to tell you how much you will make selling prints of your art. I can tell you I work hard and work long hours sometimes to make ends meet. Some months I have more than enough to pay all the bills and some months I come up short. I never said it would be easy money. The bottom line is I'm doing what I love to do and at the end of the year it all averages out.

Having said that, here are some possibilities. Examples of what you can make on the low end and on a higher end of both consignments and retail (as a street artist).

Consignments; Low end example:
Let's say you have your art prints on consignment in ten stores. Each store sells two 8x10 mat size prints per month.
Your wholesale price is;
$10.00 each
So, you make $20.00 per store. $20.00 x 10 stores

= $200.00 per month gross income from your consignments. That's $1,200.00 per year.

Consignments; Higher end example:

Let's say you have your art prints on consignment in twenty five stores. Each store sells five 8x10 mat size prints, three 11x14 mat size prints and one 16x20 mat size print per month.
Your wholesale prices are;
8x10 = $10.00 each x 5 = $50.00
11x14 = $17.50 each x 3 = $52.50
16x20 = 32.50 each x 1 = $32.50

So, you make $135.00 per store. $135.00 x 25 stores = $3,375.00 per month gross income from your consignments. That's $40,500.00 per year!

Retail sales (street artist); Low end example:

Let's say you work as a street artist three days a week, and each day you sell two 8x10 mat size prints.

Your retail price is; $20.00 each
So, you make $40.00 per day. $40.00 x 3 days = $120.00 per week x 52 weeks = $7,280.00 gross income per year.

Retail sales (street artist); Higher end example:

Let's say you work as a street artist five days a week, and each day you sell five 8x10 mat size prints, three 11x14 mat size prints, and one 16x20

mat size print.
Your retail prices are;
8x10 = $20.00 each x 5 = $100.00
11x14 = $35.00 each x 3 = $105.00
16x20 = $65.00 each x 1 = $65.00

So, you make $270.00 per day. $270.00 x 5 days =
$1,350.00 per week x 52 weeks = $70,200.00 gross
income per year!

Do you see the potential? I do, and I'm still working on mine.

Remember, that is GROSS income, not NET income, so you will have to subtract your material
expenses from the gross income amount.

The Art World

I've heard stories about how long it takes to get
accepted into galleries, and even then it can take
years for your art to catch on. Waiting for someone else to "discover" you and your art can be very
disappointing. If you want to work as a full-time
artist and make a living with your art, I suggest
you make it happen. Don't wait for the art world
to discover you, go out and start selling your own
art. In time, the art world will search you out - not
because you need them to survive, but because
now, they need you.

That's a bold statement, but it's true. Think of it
this way; The art world is all about making

money. You are out there selling your work and people are buying it, you are making money with your art and you are gaining notoriety. People who buy your art are starting to ask the galleries, "Do you carry (your name here)'s art?"

How long do you think it will take for the art world to stand and take notice? If there is money to be made selling your art, and people are asking for it, galleries will be coming to you wanting your work.

It may take years for this to happen, or it could happen in a few months. Either way, you don't care, because you are making a living with your art and doing what you love to do.

About the Author

Brian Marshall White

The author and cover artist of *Breaking into the Art World* is Marshall White.

Marshall lives in Kona, Hawaii and works as a full-time artist. His paintings and prints of Hawaii are wonderfully detailed and popular with local art buyers and tourists who visit the island. His art has been published on the cover of Multi-Hulls International magazine and in several other local island magazines and tourists guides. At this writing, his works of art are displayed in various galleries in Hawaii and in Thailand and are collected by people from all over the world.

Marshall has no formal art education, just a natural God given talent for being creative. In high school he excelled at art and wood shop, and was referred to as *"Rembrandt"* because of his natural ability as an artist. Out of high school he worked as a industrial painter, house painter and eventually settled with a career in sign painting.

As a sign writer, Marshall learned the many skills associated with producing signage, a few of which are typography, use of color, hand lettering, design and manufacturing processes, basic business and some sales skills. After becoming a vested union member in the International Brotherhood of Painters and Allied Trades, Marshall moved to Hawaii to follow a dream and work as a full-time artist.

This book is the first of his writings to be published and was written to help other artists who often ask him, "Do you make a living with your art and how did you make the jump to being a full-time artist?" It has been written for people, who like himself when he began, have no clue what do to get started marketing and selling their art.

Marshall's art can be viewed online at:
www.BrianMarshallWhite.com

Marshall White Fine Art
PO Box 1555
Kailua Kona, HI 96745-1555

Printed in the United States
37334LVS00002B/47

9 781589 397620